AF412846

THE TRANSFER SOCIETY

THE TRANSFER SOCIETY

ECONOMIC EXPENDITURES ON TRANSFER ACTIVITY

DAVID N. LABAND AND GEORGE McCLINTOCK

CATO INSTITUTE
Washington, D.C.

Library of Congress Cataloging-in-Publication Data

Laband, David N.
  The transfer society : economic expenditures on transfer activity /
David N. Laband and George McClintock.
      p. cm.
  Includes bibliographical references and index.
  ISBN 1-930865-11-2 — ISBN 1-930865-10-4 (pbk.)
  1. Income distribution—United States.   2. Subsidies—United
States.   3. Employee fringe benefits—United States.   4. Rent—United
States.   I. McClintock, George II. Title
HC110.I5 L265 2001
331.25—dc21   2001047226

Printed in the United States of America.

CATO INSTITUTE
1000 Massachusetts Ave., N.W.
Washington, D.C. 20001

We are deeply indebted to Randy Beard, Richard Beil, David Boaz, Bill Niskanen, Tom Palmer, and John Sophocleus for insightful and constructive comments.

Contents

1. INTRODUCTION — 1

2. OVERVIEW OF THE PROBLEM — 5

3. RESOURCE EXPENDITURES TO EFFECT/PREVENT *DIRECT* TRANSFERS — 21

4. RESOURCE EXPENDITURES TO EFFECT/PREVENT *INDIRECT* TRANSFERS — 41

5. WHY SO LITTLE OBSERVED RENT-SEEKING? — 53

6. CONCLUDING COMMENTS — 73

    REFERENCES — 79

    INDEX — 81

One of the great inconveniences of everyday life is locks. We get used to them but they're a pain in the neck. The great majority of us have to carry keys because of the tiny minority that brings us down to their level. We have to consider everyone a potential thief because of a few thieves.

—Andy Rooney

Generally, governments do not impose protective tariffs on their own. They have to be lobbied or pressured into doing so by the expenditure of resources in political activity. One would anticipate that the domestic producers would invest resources in lobbying for the tariff until the marginal return on the last dollar spent was equal to its likely return, which would produce a transfer. There might also be other interests trying to prevent the transfer and putting resources into influencing the government in the other direction. These expenditures, which may simply offset each other to some extent, are purely wasteful from the standpoint of society as a whole; they are spent not in increasing wealth, but in attempting to transfer or resist transfer of wealth. *I can suggest no way of measuring these expenditures, but the potential returns are large, and it would be quite surprising if the investment was not also sizable.* [emphasis added]

—Gordon Tullock

The assumption cannot be sustained that rent-seeking investments are likely to be small relative to the rents sought.

—Dennis Mueller

1. Introduction

"Principles of economics" textbooks are terribly incomplete. Virtually all of the analysis pertaining to microeconomics is confined to the behavior of "consumers" and "producers." To be sure, an understanding of why consumers make the choices they do is vitally important to an understanding of an economy, any economy. So is knowing how production is organized. Nonetheless, there is more to economic activity than producing and consuming goods and services. Specifically, individuals devote enormous amounts of time, money, and other resources to influence the distribution of income and wealth. This activity occurs in every country in the world, including (perhaps especially) the United States, and takes two forms: attempts to appropriate other persons' wealth, and attempts to prevent other people from appropriating one's own wealth. Employment of one's time and resources in pursuit of either activity may be privately rational yet socially costly, by virtue of the implied forgone opportunity to use the resources to create new products and services that are valued.

We attempt to document the magnitude of the resource expenditures associated with involuntary transfers in the United States. In chapter 2 we provide an overview of our analysis. Of particular importance is our discussion of the reason the expenditure of resources to obtain or prevent forced transfers is socially harmful, even though we acknowledge that such activity is privately rational.

In chapter 3 we present the first of two sets of numbers—estimated expenditures to arrange and prevent direct, or private, forced transfers (i.e., transfers that are not arranged through the state). We follow this up in chapter 4 with a discussion of estimated expenditures to arrange and prevent indirect (i.e., state-ordered and enforced) forced transfers. As there is a time lag associated with release of government statistics, the most recent year for which data were fully available at the time we started this project was 1997. We report that in 1997 a conservatively estimated $424 billion was spent by individuals and the state to effect or prevent involuntary direct transfers of wealth and that an additional minimum of $125 billion was spent on efforts to effect or prevent governmentally arranged (indirect) transfers of wealth. With an approximate population of 265 million in 1997, this amounts to an average expenditure of over $2,000 for every man, woman, and child in America.

These numbers reflect only the expenditures that we are able to measure or estimate reasonably accurately. As we discuss in chapter 5, there is no question but that additional expenditures occur each year; we simply are unable to measure or estimate them with any confidence. However, judging from the size of the transfers themselves (substantially more than $3 trillion in direct and indirect transfers were arranged by the federal and state governments in 1997) it would be astounding if there were not considerably more, albeit implicit, noncash investment in seeking and/or preventing forced transfers from occurring. There is every reason to believe that individuals will invest resources to obtain governmentally provided transfers. Moreover, individuals, firms, and groups that stand to lose from such transfers have clear and powerful incentives to invest resources to prevent governmentally arranged forced transfers from harming them.

In theory, such investment by all parties should take place until the expected marginal benefit, in the form of arranged or blocked transfers, exactly equals the marginal cost. But the numbers just reported do not do justice to economic theory. We have just indicated that $3 trillion worth of direct and indirect transfers were arranged through the public sector in 1997, but only $125 billion in recorded expenditures to obtain those transfers. In chapter 5 we discuss why the observed

2

resource expenditures are so small relative to the size of the known and estimated transfers. However, these resource investments are not obvious, and thus are difficult to trace.

We offer concluding comments in chapter 6.

2. Overview of the Problem

The Importance of Greed and Self-Interest

The 1980s are referred to, pejoratively, as the "decade of greed." Not that the 1980s were different than any other 10-year period in the history of humankind, with respect to the fundamental observation that individuals act in furtherance of their own self-interest. Historically, greed has been both a powerful and a pervasive motivating force. The desire to have what others have (or more than what others have) provides incentive for individuals to engage in genuinely productive economic behavior by inventing products or processes for doing things that contribute to the well-being of others. Thus do the Andrew Carnegies, Sam Waltons, and Bill Gateses of the world become exceedingly rich, while improving and enriching the lives of literally hundreds of millions of people. We concede that certain individuals suffer from the fact that Bill Gates builds a better mousetrap—namely, those who built the poorer mousetraps that his now has displaced. However, he did not intend deliberately to visit suffering upon those producers. Their hurt is a natural consequence of the fact that many millions of consumers were made better off by Gates's product(s), as compared with theirs.

The desire to have what others have also provides incentive for individuals to engage in economic behavior that is not only unproductive but unquestionably harmful to society. They devote resources to trying to acquire, directly or indirectly, the wealth of their fellow humans. As might be imagined, individuals can be remarkably creative when it comes to devising ways to appropriate someone else's wealth. We are referring, in its simplest form, to stealing. Stealing is a forced transfer from the victim to the thief. Sometimes the thief comes when no one is at home. On other occasions, the transfer is negotiated at the end of the barrel of a gun. Of much greater import than robbery and burglary, in aggregate monetary impact, are the forced transfers that are arranged in courtrooms and by local zoning boards, regulatory commissions, and legislative bodies at all levels. In every case, the perpetrators expend economic resources to effect the forced transfers. Society is worse off as a result.

The Social Cost of Forced Transfers

We offer a simple example to illustrate both the incentives and the results. Ms. Smith and Mr. Jones are prospective entrepreneurs. Smith invests $10 million worth of her time, energy, expertise, capital, and so forth to build a factory, purchase materials, hire workers, and so on that enable her to produce shoes for sale to consumers. She has sales of $11 million. The difference between revenues and costs, $1 million, represents profits for Smith. Society clearly benefits from Smith's entrepreneurial activity: as individuals voluntarily paid her $11 million (in the aggregate) for the shoes she produced, we must conclude that they valued the shoes at least that much, if not more. So, the economic activity that Smith is engaged in creates value for society that exceeds the cost of the resources employed.

Jones also invests $10 million worth of his time, energy, expertise, capital, and so on. He is a lobbyist for the National Dairymen's Association (he is really spending Association money). Through public relations efforts and judicious contributions to various congressmen, he is able to obtain federal regulation that results in artificially high milk prices that generate an additional $11 million for the dairy industry. A resource investment of $10 million has generated additional revenues of $11 million and additional profit of $1 million.

In motivation, Smith and Jones are indistinguishable. Both individuals invested $10 million with the intent of making $11 million. That is, the incentives from the perspective of the individual entrepreneur are identical. When we consider societal well-being, however, there is a fundamental difference between the activity engaged in by Smith and that engaged in by Jones. Society values the final product created by Smith's investment at a minimum of $1 million more than the investment cost. By contrast, society does not value the "product" created by Jones' investment. There are no extra goods to sell to a clamoring public. In fact, there is no new product at all for American consumers. The only result of Jones's investment is an $11 million wealth transfer from many millions of consumers of milk to a few thousand milk producers. Politicians, with support or under pressure from the milk industry, have taken advantage of American consumers to the tune of $11 million. We reiterate: Jones' resource investment leads only to a change in the distribution of income; no new product is created that consumers value.

The problem with this activity from an economic perspective is that the $10 million that Jones "invested" could have been used to produce something of real value to consumers. Obviously, it was not; $10 million spent to steal money from consumers is $10 million not spent to provide a new product that they value. We take pains to emphasize the fact that Jones's behavior is privately rational. A lot of people will spend $10 million to obtain $11 million. However, entrepreneurs who focus on redistributing wealth forgo opportunities to create real value for consumers. Consumers are the worse for it.

But the cost to society from such redistributional activity exceeds the lost productivity of the economic resources expended by those hoping to "steal" someone else's wealth. Individuals also devote economic resources in efforts to *prevent* their wealth from being appropriated by others. We buy locks and alarm systems to prevent theft. We hire lawyers and even lobbyists to protect ourselves against legal raids on our wealth. When the steel industry lobbied for restrictions on imports of foreign steel, Caterpillar (a heavy-equipment manufacturer) lobbied against such restrictions, because they raised the price of steel, which in turn raised the cost of producing earth-moving equipment. Movie theaters issue tickets and employ ticket-takers to prevent nonpayers from viewing the movies they show. Similarly with music concerts and theatrical productions. Stores employ electronic or human scanners to prevent customers from walking out with merchandise.[1]

Most of us are dimly aware, at some level, that this redistributional activity is taking place around us. We hear that politicians engage in pork barrel politics by loading down spending bills with special favors (i.e., favorable wealth redistributions) for specific interest groups in their districts. We worry about being robbed or otherwise stolen from. The state seizes property without due process or adequate compensation to the affected (former) owner(s). Tax lawyers and tax accountants find ways for clients to reduce their tax bills.

The focus of most previous empirical investigators of the welfare cost of transfer activity has been on state-ordered transfers—via regulation, tariffs, and import restrictions—of artificially contrived scarcity rents. Part of the welfare cost of transfers, especially those arranged through the state, is precisely that some portion of the transfers must be structured inefficiently to be achieved in the first place (Tullock, 1989). It is more difficult for a public official to lavish cash (taken from taxpayers, of course) on his family, friends, and supporters than it is for him to steer a few juicy state government contracts to companies owned by those individuals. The former is obvious. The latter is less visible and thus does not enrage the voter/taxpayers quite as much.

To the investigative scientist, the appealing feature of regulations and trade restrictions is that comparison to an alternative order is relatively easy to conceptualize. The welfare cost of tariffs is estimated as if the relevant alternative state is a world (or country) without tariffs. More generally, as noted by Tollison (1982), the implied alternative order is a world of zero transactions costs, which implies that efficiency-enhancing transfers would occur voluntarily and instantaneously. A

8

straightforward implication is that transfers that occur involuntarily in such a world reduce, rather than enhance, social welfare.

We take pains to emphasize that we do not assume that the transfer itself is social welfare reducing. When $100 is taken from Smith and given to Jones, the $100 is still there. With perfect information, Smith would know that she would lose in a struggle with Jones over the $100 and the money would simply be transferred. She would be poorer, but he would be richer. Thus, the aggregate effects would cancel out. However, in the presence of imperfect information and uncertainty neither Smith nor Jones can be sure who would win, so Jones invests resources in stealing the $100, while Smith invests resources to protect herself against theft. If the result of this resource expenditure is that no transfer takes place, they both end up poorer by the amount spent to affect the outcome of the struggle. It is this expenditure of resources that is costly to society, because the resources could have been employed in a truly productive capacity.

However, both Becker (1983) and Tullock (1988) have questioned whether transfer-seeking or prevention really imposes a cost, in the traditional sense of forgone opportunities, to society. They argue that rent-seeking expenditures are unavoidable, a consequence of our democratic political decisionmaking apparatus. Moreover, there is no relevant, less costly system, by virtue of the fact that we have not voted it into being. That is, transfers are conducted "efficiently." This leaves us to contemplate the possibility that there really is no welfare cost of transfer activity, as there is no relevant, more highly valued alternative to our current system of decisionmaking, with its endemic transfer activity.[2]

This argument may have merit in a static sense, but its validity in the dynamic setting in which we find ourselves seems questionable. Nobel laureate James Buchanan, for example, has written at length on the problems associated with fiscal illusion.[3] Fiscal illusion renders our existing order imperfect, but there is little, if any, chance that any other tax or spend mechanism will be adopted as a replacement for general fund financing. By the logic espoused by Becker and Tullock, fiscal illusion is not costly because there is no relevant alternative funding mechanism. However, the fact is that fiscal illusion *is* costly and we have a collective interest in knowing just how costly because, in a dynamic, long-run sense, attempts to maintain the existing order or to introduce more efficient systems may be driven, at least in part, by our knowledge about the magnitude of the costs associated with the existing order. Likewise, the cost of coal is of interest because it might stimulate entrepreneurial efforts to alter the production technology. We have an interest in the magnitude of resource expenditures related to transfer activity, as the design of future institutional arrangements may hinge on that knowledge.

As we demonstrate, investment in redistributive activity is both pervasive and extensive. The annual bill is staggeringly high—in the many hundreds of billions, if not trillions, of dollars—at a conservative estimate. This is not to argue that such efforts are inefficient, given our existing socio-legal institutions. Indeed, we suspect that redistributive activity is conducted efficiently by all parties. It is a mistake, however, to confuse the term "efficient" with the term "costless." Economists generally agree that the price system allocates goods and services efficiently, but efficiency in allocation does not occur costlessly. It is costly to define and enforce the structure of property rights that provides a foundation for our exchange economy, for example. The value of toting up the bill regarding transfer activity is that it permits us to evaluate our behavior with respect to redistributive activity, just as a periodic bar bill enables one to evaluate one's drinking behavior.

Determining the Magnitude of Redistributional Activity

Most Americans do not appreciate the sheer magnitude of the investment of economic resources devoted to redistributive activity and, thus, the extent to which this activity dampens productive economic activity. They do not appreciate the magnitude because they *cannot* appreciate the magnitude; they do not have any real understanding of just how much of this activity is taking place around them. We were heartened by the recent effort of *Time* magazine reporters Donald Barlett and James Steele (1998), who conducted an extensive 18-month study on corporate welfare in America. They estimated that the federal government provides *$125 billion a year* in subsidies to for-profit corporate entities.[4] Our purpose is to shed additional empirical light on the magnitude of the resource expenditures that pertain to redistributive activity in the U.S. economy.

As far as we know, there is no simple way of doing this. We simply cannot know, for example, exactly how much would-be burglars spend to perpetrate their crimes. Burglars and thieves know who they are, but in general we do not, so it is difficult to acquire information from them. Moreover, it seems likely that even if we were able to ask them to tell us about their expenditures of resources to carry out their burglaries they would not tell. Or, if they did tell, they would be less than truthful. And yet, we can estimate the resource investment made by burglars. We know, for example, what the average jail sentence is for those convicted of burglary, as well as the likelihood of being convicted once accused. Assuming that an individual jailed for burglary would otherwise be employed in a position that pays him at least the minimum wage, it should be clear that by choosing burglary instead, he implicitly put his future time (and earnings) at risk. That is an economic investment that we can (and do) measure.

We know how much individuals spend on tax accountants and tax attorneys each year. Their efforts influence the extent to which individual citizens retain their earnings or wealth in the face of laws and regulations requiring them to transfer their earnings or wealth to governments. Tax accountants and tax attorneys are instruments in a distributional struggle between taxpayers and governments.

We know how many contested divorces there are each year and how much, on average, is spent on attorneys in contested divorces. Divorces are not contested because one or both parties are creating some new product for society. An individual contests a divorce to influence the distribution of the assets (wealth), including access to, and parental rights over, children, accumulated during the marriage. Both parties would be better off if they could agree on a distribution of the marital assets without spending thousands of dollars on attorneys' fees, plus tens or hundreds of hours worth of their own time.

Assumptions and Methodology

Our work was guided by two important assumptions. The assumptions should be understood as applying to forced transfers, which, to us, are defined by the involuntary participation of those from whom wealth is taken, as distinct from exchanges, which are defined by the voluntary participation of all parties.

1. *A transfer is a transfer is a transfer.* We make no attempt to distinguish a dubious concept of "good" transfers as opposed to "bad" transfers.
2. *Entrepreneurs are assumed to be indifferent, ceteris paribus, between investing resources in securing/blocking transfers and investing resources in creation of positively valued product.*

Our procedure for measuring the resource investments made by individuals to effect or to prohibit forced transfers of wealth is to identify, as best we can, as many of the transfers as possible and then to track down the actual dollar expenditures made by the interested parties. That is, the task before us is akin to a many-thousand-piece, unassembled jigsaw puzzle. We attempt to construct enough of the puzzle to give viewers an appreciation for the overall picture. Where we are unable to obtain actual dollar expenditures, we provide conservative estimates.

Wherever possible, we have attempted to measure resource expenditures directly. Certain expenditures clearly have a long-run amortization period (e.g., door locks, bank vault doors, etc.), but precise knowledge of the correct period is costly to obtain. Under the circumstances, we have assumed that all relevant rates of depreciation or individuals' discount rates remain constant, in the aggregate, from year to year. That assumption permits us to pick a "representative" year, in this case 1997, and measure the full cost of locks installed in, for example, all new cars produced in the United States, without prorating that cost over the expected lifetime of the vehicles. By assumption, identical investments are forthcoming every year. The pro rata costs from previous years that would otherwise need to be figured into the 1997 figure are equal in real terms for cars produced in 1979 and for cars produced in 1997. Our typical procedure, then, was to measure specific expenditures for newly produced items in 1997.

Methodological Issues

We concede that the mere fact that individuals, acting on their own or acting collectively, are willing to invest resources to prevent others from stealing their property may, by itself, induce investment in a higher level of economically productive activity than would occur in the absence of security of private property rights. Thus it might be argued that resource investments that appear to function merely to influence distributional outcomes in fact serve a productive purpose when placed in a more encompassing context. However, the fact remains that we all would be better off if we could minimize the costs associated with forced transfers of wealth.

This raises a legitimate question of where to draw the line between resource expenditures that might be considered productive from those that are unproductive. It is generally agreed, for example, that expenditures to define and enforce property rights have a positive social payoff, since well-defined and secured property rights are a sine qua non of escape from the Hobbesian state of nature in which everyone struggles with neighbors for possession of anything of value. Definitionally, then, expenditures reduce social welfare when they are designed to reallocate property via involuntary transfer on the part of one or more of the affected parties. But the line of demarcation between socially productive and socially destructive expenditures is not obvious.

One useful distinction to make is between the definition and the enforcement of property rights. Measuring the resource expenditures on socially costly redistributive activity can only proceed from an existing order, characterized by a prevailing distribution of defined property rights. The expenditure of resources to define individual rights to property clearly is socially beneficial, if for no other reason than that it helps minimize negative externalities resulting from unintended infringement. However, enforcement of property rights is necessary only insofar as there is less-than-unanimous agreement with the distribution of defined property rights and, as noted previously, positive transactions costs. In our example, Smith and Jones fight only when they are unsure about the outcome of the struggle to control the wealth. In principle, enforcement against involuntary transfers can be produced privately or publicly, with the only rationale for the latter being some sort of economy of scale. If everyone obeys the dictum "Thou shalt not steal," there is no need for police, jails, and locks.

One way of approaching the measurement problem, then, is to start from a perfect world in which property rights were well-defined and agreed on by everyone. In such a world, there would be no involuntary transfers (i.e., no theft), and the cost of enforcing against involuntary transfers in the world in which we actually find ourselves properly would be included as a cost of involuntary transfer activity. A second way of approaching the measurement problem is to assume that the relevant comparison state is a world with perfect information, thus no uncertainty. Such a world may be characterized by involuntary transfers, but they would be costless in the sense that they would be effected without the expenditure of resources by either party, as in our Smith and Jones example. In this case, expenditures on enforcement of existing property rights in the world in which we find ourselves are properly regarded as socially productive and should not be counted in our tally. The reason is that property rights that are transferred involuntarily imply that value has, on balance, been destroyed. Smith values her car at $10,000, even though the book value of the car is only $5,000. When Jones steals the car and receives $500 from a chop shop, there has been a net reduction in social welfare. Expenditures made by Smith to protect against her welfare being lowered are privately rational and socially productive. Note, however, that this interpretation is an artifact of the differing values placed by Smith and Jones on the item(s) potentially or actually transferred.

Our general approach is to assume an existing distribution of property rights and argue that investments in attempts to *reallocate* those rights are socially wasteful when any of the affected parties participates involuntarily. Property rights to Smith's car are reallocated to Jones when she sells her car to him. Both parties participate in the exchange voluntarily. This makes both parties better off than before the transaction. However, when Jones steals Smith's car, Smith "participates" in the reallocation of property rights involuntarily. The forced transfer is welfare-reducing; resources expended by either Smith or Jones to affect the outcome are wasted because they could have been put to productive use.

Let us be specific. How do we treat fences, titles to property, and locks? We make a general distinction between actions taken initially to define and enforce property rights (or to voluntarily redefine those rights) and those designed to redistribute existing rights involuntarily. Expenditure of economic resources on activities that influence the forced redistribution of property rights that already are well-defined and enforced clearly is socially wasteful. When "the law" recognizes and ostensibly protects our legal rights to "our" property, the money we nevertheless spend for locks, safety deposit boxes, and so forth represents dead-weight loss. So we regard titles, registrations, title insurance, and the like as reasonable baseline expenditures that help define ownership rights to physical property, deviations from which are wealth reducing. Similarly with respect to patents, copyrights, and trademarks that define ownership of intellectual property.

We consider the primary purpose of fences to be the definition of an individual's property rights. Even though the state may recognize Mr. Brown's legal rights to his physical property and enforce those rights by means of laws against trespass, such trespass may occur accidentally by virtue of the encroacher's ignorance of the precise boundaries. That is, there would be no encroachment if the boundaries to Brown's property were clearly visible. In defining the boundaries visibly by means of a fence, the owner minimizes unintended takings (use) by others.

We concede that fences may reduce theft and that by failing to account for this we likely bias downward our estimate of the resource expenditure on transfer activity. However, we suspect that any such bias is small. In contrast, locks requiring keys or special combinations normally protect against intentional, rather than unintentional, takings of property.

What Do the Numbers Look Like?

The numbers are staggering: we estimate that Americans expended *a minimum of $400 billion* worth of economic resources in 1997 to influence the distribution of wealth. There is good reason to suspect that the expenditures are, in reality, much, much greater. The total amount of wealth affected by direct and indirect transfer activity in 1997 easily exceeded $3 *trillion*. Our findings are important for two reasons: First, they reveal that a significant amount of economic activity in the United States is redistributive in purpose and effect, rather than productive. That is, the expenditures reflect fighting over the existing economic pie as opposed to baking a larger economic pie. Second, the overtly observable investments to obtain forced transfers from others and investments to prevent others from forcibly taking wealth apparently constitute a relatively small fraction of the total wealth at stake.

We have included in our analysis *every* expenditure (that we can identify specifically or otherwise estimate) that is associated with forced transfers, without regard to more encompassing philosophical questions about the proper role of the state. For example, we have included public sector expenditures for police protection against burglary, robbery, and theft. By the same logic, we have included certain expenditures for the United States military. That is, local police help protect against theft directed at individuals (American-on-American theft); the U.S. military helps protect against non-Americans taking the wealth of Americans, considered collectively. We also identify an array of private expenditures intended to prevent theft.

Our Numbers Understate the Magnitude of the Problem

The numbers contained in this analysis understate the true amount of investment in redistributive activity, perhaps substantially. We are unable to effectively measure certain investments; thus we do not include them in our estimates. To take but one case in point, consider safe deposit boxes. We know that millions of safe deposit boxes are rented each year in America. However, we have no way of tracking down just exactly what this number is (we've tried). At rental fees that probably range between $30 and $75 per year, we are unable to measure a resource expenditure that likely is several hundred million dollars annually. More insidiously, we know that individuals and groups who seek special favors from elected politicians, unelected bureaucrats, or both at all levels of government expend resources to "convince" these officials to provide special favors. Such de facto bribery only occasionally, not typically, involves cash payments; cash is obvious. Instead, seekers of special wealth transfers from representatives or employees of the state have found myriad noncash ways to purchase political favors:

- take the local political representative to lunch at a classy restaurant, seeker's treat

- treat him to golf at the local exclusive club
- patronize her law firm with other business; because she is a partner, she gets a share of the resulting net revenues
- invite her to be the featured (and richly rewarded) speaker at your organization's annual meeting
- treat him to the suite life at the local NFL, semipro, or major-college football or basketball stadium
- sell him some prime development acreage at fire sale prices—let him resell it for a bundle
- make a large contribution to the John Q. Senator Institute for Statesmanship at the local university in his state
- make a large donation to his favorite charity, on whose board of directors he or his spouse probably sits
- arrange a full college scholarship for one or more of her children
- arrange for an attractive escort to spend time with him.

The Olympics bribery scandal of early 1999 provided a plethora of real-life examples of sub rosa payoffs designed to influence selection committee members charged with determining the sites of Olympic games. The payoffs clearly did not produce anything of value to consumers.

Distortions in the Economy

Clearly, the pattern of production of certain goods and services in the U.S. economy has been distorted by these redistribution-related expenditures. This was demonstrated only too clearly by Mixon, Laband, and Ekelund (1994), who showed that the number of golf courses and sit-down restaurants per capita is significantly greater in state capitals than in randomly paired, same-state cities. It is quite certain that large, defense-related firms have deliberately built production facilities in several states (rather than in one location) as a means of maximizing political support for defense spending. It is not at all clear that optimal production requires that plants be spread out like this. We have more lawyers per capita, *by a large margin*, than every other industrialized country in the world.

Only too obviously, the large number of lawyers that we have is not essential for industrial production in the United States to flourish. Lawyers are, however, instrumental in the tort process.

Measured Gross Domestic Product Overstates Productive Economic Activity

A basic problem is that, to some extent, expenditures on restaurants, golf courses, lawyers, alcohol, tax accountants, safe deposit boxes, keyed ignitions for vehicles, door locks, and other economic resources employed in the wealth redistribution process are counted as part of gross domestic product (GDP). That is, these products or services are treated in the national accounting statistics as if they produce something that truly adds to the well-being of society. In fact, these expenditures do not lead to production of goods or services that increase the welfare of American citizens. This implies that *measured* GPD overstates the *actual* level of productive (i.e., socially valued) economic activity in the U.S. economy.

Organization of Chapters

In chapters 3 and 4 we present the numbers. Resource expenditures used to protect against or perpetrate direct, person-to-person transfers are identified in chapter 3, by type of expenditure. We identify resource expenditures on indirect transfers, which involve the state, in chapter 4. In both chapters, we present the resource expenditure figures first, followed by corresponding information on our sources.

Notes

1. Varian (1989) specifically addresses the welfare implications of theft, taxation, and monopoly. His discussion of theft (p. 82) is relevant to our measurement of expenditures on locks, and so forth: "In a partial equilibrium setting theft appears to be a purely redistributive activity that therefore involves no deadweight loss. However, upon reflection it is clear that considerable economic resources are devoted to the *prevention* of theft. Thus, any computation of the dead-weight burden of changes in government policy towards theft such as a change in the level of law enforcement, must include

not only the direct expenditures on law enforcement, but also the indirect effects of changes in demand and supply for locks, alarms, insurance, etc." (Italics his) There is a curious one-sidedness to Varian's argument, because he neglects to mention the obvious expenditure of resources (principally labor) by would-be thieves. Similarly, although he subsequently recognizes that individuals will invest resources to evade taxes and to acquire monopolies, he overlooks the investment of resources by individuals opposed to the formation of a monopoly by some other party. The incentive to oppose such efforts and the resulting resource investments are nontrivial. The automotive manufacturers have significant financial incentive to oppose efforts by steel producers to cartelize the steel industry or to restrict imports of foreign-manufactured steel. Peltzman (1976) offers the first formal model of the manner in which individuals opposed to wealth transfers to special interest groups influence public policy. Additional discussion of the resource investment by individuals and groups opposed to proposed wealth transfers is contained in Tollison (1982) and Becker (1983).

2. This conundrum did not escape Jensen and Meckling (1976). They note (pp. 327–28): "The reduced value of the firm caused by the manager's consumption of perquisites outlined above is 'nonoptimal' or inefficient only in comparison to a world in which we could obtain compliance of the agent to the principal's wishes at zero cost or in comparison to a hypothetical world in which the agency costs were lower. But these costs (monitoring and bonding costs and 'residual loss') are an unavoidable result of the agency relationship."

3. Fiscal illusion occurs when individuals do not have an accurate understanding of the tax prices they pay for publicly provided goods and services. Specifically, they underestimate the true tax prices, which causes them to demand more of the associated public goods and services than they would have demanded in possession of more accurate tax price information. See especially Buchanan (1967) (pp. 126–43). See also Buchanan and Tullock (1962), Buchanan (1968), and Buchanan and Brennan (1980).

4. This is consistent with Stephen Moore and Dean Stansel (1995), who reported that more than $85 billion of taxpayers' money was spent in fiscal year 1995 on "more than 125 federal programs that subsidize private businesses."

3. Resource Expenditures to Effect/ Prevent *Direct* Transfers

Introduction

In this chapter we report our findings with respect to resource investment in the United States related to *direct*, person-to-person transfer activity. That is, our focus is on situations in which Smith attempts personally to appropriate Jones's property, against Jones's wishes. Burglary, for example, clearly falls into this category, as does robbery. However, when Smith attempts to employ the takings power of the state, as opposed to a gun, to rob Jones, the transfer is indirect. Smith gets others (e.g., politicians) to do her dirty work for her. We postpone until chapter 4 our analysis of indirect forced transfers.

In this chapter, we identify expenditures made by individuals who seek to transfer wealth from others directly to themselves and expenditures made by individuals who seek to *prevent* their wealth from being taken from them without their consent. In some cases, the resource expenditures are explicit—for example, when an individual purchases a home safe for $1,500 to prevent a burglar from stealing her jewelry. However, a significant portion of the resource expenditure is implicit—for example, the value of the time spent by an individual in planning and carrying out a burglary.

We identify three principal categories of resource expenditures: (1) investments by the state to protect against illegal (forced) wealth transfers, (2) investments by private parties to protect against illegal wealth transfers, and (3) investments by private parties to perpetrate illegal wealth transfers.

Investments by the State to Protect against *Illegal* Wealth Transfers

ORGANIZED CRIME

Organized crime investigations (FBI)	$281,535,000
Labor racketeering (Department of Labor)	11,253,000
Subtotal	$292,788,000

WHITE COLLAR CRIME

Government fraud (General Accounting Office)	$332,261,000
Mail fraud (FBI)	6,044,400
(U.S. Postal Service)	45,982,608
Program fraud (Department of Labor)	8,251,000
Subtotal	$392,539,008

INVESTIGATIONS OF PERSONAL CRIMES

Bank robbery and related crimes	$96,710,400
Subtotal	$96,710,400

NATIONAL DEFENSE $154,000,000,000

POLICE

Police protection	$16,650,000,000
Corrections	12,765,000,000
Judicial/legal	3,783,948,700
Subtotal	$33,198,948,700

PROTECTION AGAINST RESTRAINT OF TRADE/FRAUD

Federal Trade Commission	$47,437,000
Securities and Exchange Commission	104,618,000
Subtotal	$152,055,000

Investments by Private Parties to Protect against *Illegal* Wealth Transfers

RESIDENTIAL INVESTMENTS

Locks—Vehicles

Passenger cars	$2,401,383,320
Light trucks	2,225,454,200
Medium to heavy trucks	113,515,000
Motor homes	22,385,000
Travel trailers, folding camping trailers, truck camper shells	8,379,000
Subtotal	$4,771,166,520

Locks—"After-Market" Locking Devices

"The Club"	$180,000,000
Security straps	105,608,000
Subtotal	$285,608,000

Locks—Houses/Apartments

Privately owned, 1-family houses	$101,007,000
Privately owned, 2- to 4-unit housing	1,472,400
Privately owned, 5+ unit housing	4,878,000
Mobile homes	5,754,600
Apartment mailboxes	1,497,200
Subtotal	$114,609,200

Locks—Miscellaneous

Suitcase locks	$186,590,000
Gun safes	95,000,000
Lawn mower locks	120,232,000
Boat locks	8,154,000
Snowmobile locks	3,256,520
Motorcycle locks	35,600,000
Subtotal	$478,832,520

Insurance

Underwriting expenses for private insurance
premiums paid in 1997 for

Burglary/theft	$ 36,670,636
Auto liability	19,099,405,000
Homeowner's multiple peril	7,288,653,400
Subtotal	$26,424,728,036

Burglar Alarms	$5,740,000,000
Auto Security	$325,000,000
Time	$10,494,080,000

COMMERCIAL INVESTMENTS

Locks—Vehicles	$155,553,800

Locks—Buildings/Offices/Desks

Buildings	$36,800,000
Churches	6,235,629
Hotel rooms	39,460,290
Subtotal	$82,495,919

Commercial Corporate, Government, and Institutional Security	$71,880,000,000
Retail Inventory Control	$9,756,747,000

Insurance

Underwriting expenses for commercial
insurance premiums paid in 1997 for

Auto liability	$ 3,464,378,400
Farmowner's multiple peril	368,758,100
Nonauto liability	5,443,893,257

Medical malpractice	1,320,973,920
Commercial multiple peril	5,136,258,664
Workers Compensation	6,504,733,326
Surety and fidelity	976,671,263
Financial guaranty	836,222,530
Subtotal	$24,051,889,460

Miscellaneous

Computer security	$220,665,600
Retail security (electronic article surveillance)	
	1,866,666,667
Vault doors (financial institutions)	43,179,280
Armored car services	1,200,000,000
Subtotal	$,330,511,547

Investments by Private Parties to Perpetrate *Illegal* Wealth Transfers

Burglary*	$4,483,078,700
Robbery*	3,248,905,600
Larceny/theft*	13,400,081,000
Motor vehicle theft*	1,816,829,700
*Implied risk assessment	
Subtotal	$22,948,895,200

TOTAL	$369,593,823,910

Sources

Investments by the State to Protect against *Illegal* Wealth Transfers

ORGANIZED CRIME
Organized Crime Investigations (FBI)

The fiscal year 1997 budget of the FBI was $2,628,000,000 (telephone conversation with FBI employee Celeste Smith on November 12, 1998). Organized crime investigations commanded 10.7 percent of the total FBI effort in 1997 (telephone conversation with Christie

Ryan on November 13, 1998). Thus, we estimate expenditures on organized crime investigations by multiplying the total budget of the FBI for 1997 by the fraction of FBI effort devoted to organized crime investigations: .107 × $2,628,000,000 = $281,535,000.

Labor Racketeering (Department of Labor)
This figure was provided by Ann Ahern, who works in the Office of the Inspector General, U.S. Department of Labor (by fax, February 3, 1999) and was taken from the Department's FY 1997 budget.

WHITE COLLAR CRIME
Government Fraud (General Accounting Office)
The GAO audits and evaluates the expenditure of federal funds to guard against fraud. The 1997 budget was provided by India Jenkins, Budget Director of the GAO (Telephone conversation, March 1, 1999).

Mail Fraud (FBI)
According to FBI employee Amy York (telephone conversation on December 1, 1998), expenditures on mail fraud consumed .23 percent of the FBI budget in 1997. The total FBI budget in 1997 was $2,628,000,000. Therefore, to estimate the amount expended by the FBI in 1997 on mail fraud, we multiply .0023 × $2,628,000,000 = $6,044,400.

Mail Fraud (U.S. Postal Service)
Jane Eyre at the U.S. Postal Inspection Service provided us with information on mail fraud investigation in fiscal year 1997. The expenditure of $45,982,608 represents 538,375 staff hours of investigation at the investigative hourly rate of $85.41.

Program Fraud (Department of Labor)
This figure was provided by Ahern, in the Office of the Inspector General, U.S. Department of Labor (by fax, February 3, 1999) and was taken from the Department's FY 1997 budget.

INVESTIGATIONS OF PERSONAL CRIMES
Bank robbery and related crimes absorbed 3.68 percent of the FBI's budget in 1997. Thus, we estimate expenditures on organized crime investigations by multiplying the total budget of the FBI for 1997 by the fraction of FBI effort devoted to organized crime investigations: .0368 × $2,628,000,000 = $96,710,400.

NATIONAL DEFENSE

This number was taken from Earl C. Ravenal's (1998) analysis of minimum defense expenditures required to safeguard Americans' domestic security against attack from foreigners. His estimate of $154 billion to accomplish the result stands in contrast to a 1997 defense budget of $253 billion.

POLICE

Police Protection and Corrections, Jails, and Prisons

Of the 15,284,300 arrests made in 1997, at least 2,835,450 involved transfer activity: robbery, burglary, larceny-theft, motor vehicle theft, forgery, counterfeiting, fraud, embezzlement, and stolen property (Federal Bureau of Investigation, *Uniform Crime Reports—1997*). We assume that the percentage of resources allocated by law enforcement personnel toward the handling of these cases equals the ratio of these cases to total cases (0.185). *Security* magazine was our source for total expenditures on police protection ($90 billion) and corrections, jails, and prisons ($69 billion). Information on federal expenditures on judicial/litigative activities was taken from the U.S. Bureau of Justice Statistics, *Sourcebook of Criminal Justice Statistics, 1997*.

Our estimate of expenditures on police protection involving forced transfers is derived by multiplying the fraction of all crimes that involved forced transfers (0.185) times total expenditures on police protection: $0.185 \times \$90$ billion $= \$16.65$ billion.

Similarly, our estimate of expenditures on corrections, jails and prisons involving forced transfers is derived by multiplying 0.185 times total expenditures on corrections, jails and prisons: $0.185 \times \$69$ billion $= \$12.765$ billion.

Judicial/Legal

Our estimate of expenditures on judicial/litigative activities involving forced transfers is derived by multiplying 0.185 time total expenditures on judicial/litigative activities (found at www.census.gov/govs/estimate/96stlus.txt):

$$0.185 \times \$20,453,777,000 = \$3,783,948,700.$$

PROTECTION AGAINST RESTRAINT OF TRADE/FRAUD

Federal Trade Commission

Budget figures for the Federal Trade Commission were provided by the Budget Branch Financial Management Office at their Web site (www.ftc.gov). FTC appropriations for 1997 were $102,180,000. The Competition Mission appropriations for 1997 were $47,437,000 (this information was provided by Ms. Judy Galvin in the Budget Office, per telephone conversation on October 28, 1998).

Securities and Exchange Commission

Budget figures for the Securities and Exchange Commission (SEC) were taken from the SEC Web site (www.sec.gov). The outlay for the Commission was $305 million in 1997. The expenditures that were earmarked for prevention and suppression of fraud were $104,618,000 (these figures were provided by the comptroller office of the SEC on October 28, 1998).

Investments by Private Parties to Protect against *Illegal* Wealth Transfers

RESIDENTIAL INVESTMENTS

Locks—Vehicles

The American Automobile Manufacturers Association provided data on motor vehicle production in 1997: passenger cars (5,927,000), light trucks (5,858,000), medium to heavy trucks (311,000). Total vehicle production was (12,096,000). Information on the number of units sold in 1997 of recreational vehicles was provided by Recreational Vehicle Industry Association employee, Jeff Beddow (telephone conversation and fax communication, February 5, 1999).

Passenger cars were assumed to have, on average, 6 locks: one on each front door, the ignition, the glove box, the interior hood release, and the trunk. Trucks were assumed to have 5 locks: the ignition, two door locks, interior hood release, and glovebox. Motor homes were assumed to have 4 locks: the ignition, two front door locks and one rear door lock. Travel trailers, folding camping trailers, and truck camper shells were assumed to have one lock each. In addition, the motorized vehicles were assumed to have an inside hood release mechanism. Specific prices on the lock and cylinder assemblies and the hood release cable were obtained from Auburn Ford, Lincoln-Mercury. For passenger cars, specific prices were averaged for the Crown Victoria, Contour, and Taurus, to obtain a per vehicle cost of locks. For light trucks, sport utility vehicles, and minivans, specific prices were averaged for the F-150 and Explorer. The (average) lock prices we used are

Ignition	$124.00
Glove compartment	7.45
Trunk lock	12.63

Inside hood release	16.50
Lock cylinders	21.00
Electronic locking system	18.00

As the prices reflected only replacement cost of the parts and did not include the cost of drilling holes, ignition hook-ups, installation, wiring, or keys, we assumed that these various dimensions of installation cost exactly as much again as the cost of the parts. Total cost of locks per automotive category was determined by multiplying the number of units produced by the per unit cost of locks (installed):

Passenger cars:
$$5,927,000 \times 2 \times (124.00 + 7.45 + 12.63 + 16.50 + 42.00)$$
$$= \$2,401,383,320$$

Light trucks:
$$5,858,000 \times 2 \times (124.00 + 7.45 + 16.50 + 42.00) = \$2,225,454,200$$

Medium to heavy trucks:
$$311,000 \times 2 \times (124.00 + 16.50 + 42.00) = \$113,515,000$$

Motor homes:
$$55,000 \times 2 \times (124.00 + 16.50 + 63.00) = \$22,385,000$$

Travel trailers, folding camping trailers, truck camper shells:
$$199,500 \times 2 \times 21.00 = \$8,379,000$$

Locks—"After-Market" Locking Devices
Information on 1997 revenues for "the Club" was provided by Brian Wildman, brand manager for "the Club" at Winner International, which manufactures "the Club" (telephone conversation on February 19, 1999). Wildman also provided the information on 1997 revenues from security straps.

Locks—Houses/Apartments

Privately owned, 1-family houses	1996 new units:	1,161,000
Privately owned, 2- to 4-unit housing	1996 new units:	45,000
Privately owned, 5+ unit housing	1996 new units:	271,000
Mobile Homes	1996 new units:	319,700

We assume an average of three locks per single-family house, two locks per duplex unit, and one lock each on apartments and mobile homes. The cost of an exterior door lock for houses was estimated at $29 and for apartments and mobile homes at $18 (telephone conversation with Dallas Brooks of American Lock and Key on April 28, 1999). For the new construction listed above, the calculations are

1,161,000 × 3 × $29 = $101,007,000.
45,000 × .368 (the estimated fraction of duplexes) × 2 × $29
   = $960,480
45,000 × .632 (the estimated fraction of 3-4 unit housing) × 1 ×
   $18 = $511,920
271,000 × 1 × $18 = $4,878,000
319,700 × 1 × $18 = $5,754,600

Expenditures on locks for mailboxes for apartments are calculated as follows:

Total number of apartments constructed in 1997 (from above): 299,440. The average lock price of $15 was provided by Tom Southard of S.B.S. (telephone conversation on April 15, 1999). The cost range for what he termed "vertical" and "horizontal" locks was $10–$15. The estimated cost of a "pedestal" lock was $25. Approximately 80 percent of mailbox locks are vertical or horizontal, with the remaining 20 percent being pedestal locks.

We assume that one-third of all apartments have locking mailboxes. Thus, the expenditure on locks for these mailboxes is estimated at: $15 × 299,440/3 = $1,497,200.

Locks—Miscellaneous

Suitcase Locks

For 1997, unit sales of luggage and business cases (including computers) were 32,129,000 and 9,790,000, respectively (Georgetown Economic Services). A representative from Travelpro provided information on lock pricing for luggage (telephone conversation on November 4, 1998). The most popular (middle of the road) unit has a retail price of $2.00. The top of the line unit has a retail price of $6.00. We assumed that luggage came with $2.00 locks (2) and that business cases were equipped with $6.00 locks (1). The total cost of locks was calculated as

luggage:	32,129,000 × $2.00 × 2	= $128,516,000
business cases:	9,790,000 × $6.00	= $ 58,074,000.

Gun Safes

Information was provided by Chris O'Neill, company representative for Liberty Safes (telephone conversation on June 4, 1999).

Lawn Mower Locks

The number of front-engine lawn tractors shipped in 1997 was 1,162,000. The number of garden tractors shipped in 1997 was

30

173,000. The number of commercial riding rotary turf mowers shipped in 1997 was 52,400. This information was provided by Deere & Co. employee Heather Robinson (telephone conversation on December 1, 1998). The keyed ignition switch for a Snapper rear engine riding lawn-mower costs $5.00. The cost on a front engine Snapper tractor ignition was $10.25. (Information provided by David Lee of the Auburn Rental Center, telephone conversation on November 30, 1998.) Total expenditures on keyed ignitions for riding lawn mowers were estimated at $10.25 × 1,162,000 plus $5 × (173,000 + 52,400) = $13.037,500 ($11,910,500 + 1,127,000).

Boat Locks

According to John Rustin (telephone conversation on November 30, 1998) at Action Marine, the price for a 1997 Johnson/Evinrude ignition switch was $28.95. The price for a Mercury ignition switch was $25–$30. The price for a Yamaha-manufactured switch was $35.00. According to the National Marine Manufacturers Association (Web site), the number of outboard motors sold in 1997 was 302,000. Given the range of ignition prices identified, we base our numbers on a conservative estimated average price of $27.00. To obtain an estimate of the total resource expenditure on ignition switches we multiply the $27.00 ignition switch cost times the number of units sold:

$$\$27 \times 302,000 = \$8,154,000.$$

Snowmobile Locks

According to Jaime Carter (telephone conversation on December 1, 1998) at AL's Snowmobile Parts Warehouse, the ignition switch prices for the 1997 Articat was $18.14. The price for the Yamaha model was $25.00, and the price for the Polaris switch was $19.95. According to the International Snowmobile Industry Association, the number of snowmobiles sold domestically in 1997 was 162,826. Based on the range of ignition switch prices indicated, we use an estimated average price of $20. To obtain an estimate of the total resource expenditure on ignition switches we multiply the $20.00 ignition cost times the number of units sold:

$$\$20 \times 162,826 = \$3,256,520.$$

Motorcycle Locks

Chris Felton of Honda Motorcycles in Opelika, Alabama (telephone conversation on December 2, 1998), provided ignition switch prices for 1997 model year Honda and Suzuki Motorcycles. These prices ranged from $100 to125.00. Felton also provided ignition switch information for all terrain vehicles (ATVs); the price range was $75.00–$100. The 1997 Motorcycle Industry Council Sales Report provided data on new motorcycle unit sales. An estimated 356,000 new motorcycles were sold in the U.S in 1997. We assume, conservatively, that all motorcycle ignition switch prices are $100.00. To calculate the estimated expenditure in 1997 on motorcycle ignition switches, we multiply the ignition switch price ($100) by the number of units sold that year:

$$\$100.00 \times 356,000 = \$35,600,000.$$

Insurance

In 1997, premiums paid by individuals for liability protection and protection against burglary/theft equaled

Burglary/theft	$ 135,316,000
Auto liability	70,477,508,000
Homeowner's multiple peril	26,895,400,000.

Underwriting expenses constituted 27.1 percent of the premiums received. Multiplying this percentage to the above-cited premium figures yields the amount of total premiums that we regard as 100 percent wasted.

Burglary/theft	$ 36,670,636
Auto liability	19,099,405,000
Homeowner's multiple peril	7,288,653,400

These numbers were provided by the Insurance Information Institute (by fax on October 27, 1998), taken from the *1999 Fact Book*.

Burglar Alarms

According to the SDM Industry Forecast Study, $4.9 billion was spent in 1997 on residential sales and installation, with an additional $0.84 billion spent on "home systems."

Auto Security

This information was provided by Mr. Ken Gammage (telephone conversation on November 20, 1998) of Directed Electronics, the largest provider of car security systems in the United States.

Time

We assumed that each adult (age 18 and over) in the United States spent an average of 1 minute per day dealing with vehicle locks, suitcase locks, ignitions for a large variety of vehicles (which are locks—keyed ignitions are not needed to start vehicles; an unkeyed switch will complete the required electrical circuit) insurance, alarm systems, safe deposit boxes, titles, and so forth. We valued the time spent at the median hourly pay of wage and salary workers in the United States ($8.63). There were approximately 200 million adults in the United States in 1997; the calculation is straightforward:

$$\$8.63 \times 200{,}000{,}000 \times 1/60 \times 365 = \$10{,}494{,}080{,}000.$$

COMMERCIAL INVESTMENTS

Locks—Vehicles

	Produced in 1997
Earth-moving machinery	
Articulated haulers	995
Backhoe loaders	30,975
Crawler dozers	9,570
Crawler loaders	500
Hydraulic excavators	14,400
Ditchers/trenchers	13,800
Motor graders	6,500
Rigid haulers	1,725
Scrapers	1,100
Skid-steer loaders	65,400
Wheel loaders	16,830
Subtotal	161,795
Material handling and lifting machinery	
Aerial work platform	62,100
Rough terrain lift trucks	10,225
Hydraulic cranes	2,005
Cable cranes	115
Industrial lift trucks	125,100
Subtotal	206,545
Other machinery	
Wheeled log skidders	3,110
Wheeled feller bunchers	1,105
Wheeled harvesters	80
Wheeled forwarders	275

Farm tractors	87,000
Harvesting combines	16,000
Total	106,580
Other commercial vehicles	
Fire engines	5,021
Buses	Not available
Garbage trucks	18,300
Ambulances	5,500
Truck tractors	271,539
Tugboats	200
Transport aircraft	374
Helicopters	346
General aviation	1,569
Subtotal	302,849
TOTAL	777,769

Information on the number of heavy equipment vehicles produced in 1997 was taken from Off-Highway Research, *The Construction Equipment Industry in North America: Long-Term Machinery Forecast, 1999*. According to Lester Killebrew, president of Henry Farm Center (telephone conversation on February 11, 1999), the approximate cost of an ignition unit for a tractor or combine was $200. We assume that this cost also is applicable for the other types of heavy equipment and commercial vehicles listed.

Information on the number of fire trucks produced in 1997 was provided by Al Burnham, president of the Firemen Apparatus Manufacturers' Association (telephone conversation on February 11, 1999). In 1997, a total of 5,021 new fire trucks was shipped.

Information on the approximate number of garbage trucks manufactured in 1997 was provided by Jack Legler, from the Waste Equipment Technology Association (telephone conversation on May 27, 1999).

Information on the number of ambulances produced in 1997 was provided by Mark VanArnam of American Emergency Vehicles (telephone conversation on May 5, 1999).

There were 374 transport aircraft produced in 1997, 346 helicopters manufactured in that year, and 1,569 general aviation aircraft manufactured. This information was provided by Aerospace Industries

Association employee Terry Ruby (by e-mail correspondence, February 4, 1999).

We assume that the only locking mechanism that secures the various types of commercial equipment we have identified is the ignition, with an estimated cost of $200. The estimated aggregate expenditure on ignitions for these vehicles is calculated as

$$\$200 \times 777{,}769 = \$155{,}553{,}800.$$

Locks—Buildings/Offices/Desks

As we were unable to determine the number of new office buildings constructed in 1997, we estimated the investment in locks by assuming a 20-year straight-line depreciation for the locks on all commercial buildings. The number of commercial buildings in the United States in 1995 was approximately 4,579,000 (*Statistical Abstract of the United States, 1997*, Table 1214). No doubt, the number of commercial buildings in 1997 was somewhat higher, say 4,600,000. Lock pricing data were provided by a representative from American Lock and Key (telephone conversation on November 17, 1998). Most medium grade commercial locks are priced at around $80. Commercial magnetic back door locking mechanisms cost about $1,300. The deadbolt on the door with the magnetic mechanism is an additional $50. We used the $80.00 figure, to be conservative. We assume a minimum (and an average) of two doors per commercial building. The estimated expenditure on locks is

$$(4{,}600{,}000 \times \$80 \times 2) / 20 = \$36{,}800{,}000.$$

The number of churches in the United States in 1995 was approximately 328,191 (*Statistical Abstract of the United States, 1997*, Table 85). The lock on an exit door of a church has an average price of $300.00, whereas the front door lock price has an average price of $80. The estimated expenditure on locks is

$$(328{,}191 \times \$380) / 20 = \$6{,}235{,}629.$$

According to Rob Stern at the American Hotel and Motel Association (telephone conversation on November 18, 1998), there were 202,361 newly constructed hotel and motel rooms in 1997. The typical cost of a hotel room door lock runs from $80 to $100. We split the difference and assumed an average cost of $90 per lock. Card entry locks for hotel rooms have an average price of $300. The ratio of keyed doors to card entry doors in new construction is approximately 50/50. The estimated expenditure on locks is

$$(101,180 \times \$90) + (101,180 \times \$300) = \$39,460,290.$$

Commercial, Corporate, Government, and Institutional Security
This number was developed from figures provided to us by the SDM 1998 Industry Forecast Study and *Security* magazine (faxed to us November 9, 1998). This study identifies total revenues for the private security industry in 1997 at approximately $80 billion. Of this, $5.74 billion came from residential sales and installation of burglar alarm systems (which is listed separately in this report under residential investments) and $2.38 billion came from fire alarms, which we did not include. According to the SDM Industry Forecast Study, in 1997 $3.6 billion was spent on electronic security products and services by businesses. Items included in this total are such things as commercial burglar alarm systems, guards, access control gates, surveillance cameras, and the like.

Retail Inventory Control
This information was derived from the Executive Summary to the 1998 National Retail Security Survey conducted by the University of Florida. Total retail sales in 1997 were $2.4453 trillion (*Statistical Abstract of the United States, 1998*). Respondents to the Survey indicated that on average their loss prevention budgets equaled 0.57 percent of their firms' annual retail sales. To estimate industrywide expenditures to control what the industry terms "shrinkage," we multiplied total retail sales in 1997 ($2.4453 trillion) by 0.0057, which equals $13,938,210,000. The breakdown in these expenses is as follows: 51.9 percent to payroll and benefits, 17.3 percent to contract services, 13.3 percent to "other" expenses, 12.5 percent to new capital purchases, and 5.1 percent to capital depreciation. It seems likely that contract services and new capital purchases are included in the expense recorded previously under the heading Commercial, Corporate, Government, and Institutional Security. To avoid double-counting, we subtracted an additional 30 percent for the contract services and new capital purchases, which gives us an estimate of $9,756,747,000.

Insurance
In 1997, premiums paid by businesses for liability protection equaled:

Auto liability	$12,783,684,000
Farmowner's multiple peril	1,360,731,000
Nonauto liability	20,088,167,000
Medical malpractice	4,892,496,000
Commercial multiple peril	18,952,984,000
Workers Compensation	24,002,706,000
Surety and fidelity	3,603,953,000
Financial guaranty	3,085,692,000

These numbers were provided by the Insurance Information Institute (by fax on October 27, 1998), taken from the *1999 Fact Book*.

As with residential insurance, the underwriting expenses are complete losses to society. We again multiply the fraction of underwriting expenses to premiums received in 1997 (.271) to obtain the underwriting losses:

Auto liability	$3,464,378,400
Farmowner's multiple peril	368,758,100
Nonauto liability	5,443,893,257
Medical malpractice	1,320,973,920
Commercial multiple peril	5,136,258,664
Workers Compensation	6,504,733,326
Surety and fidelity	976,671,263
Financial guaranty	836,222,530

Miscellaneous

Computer Security

Network Associates is a leading provider of anti-virus software products and network security products. According to their 1997 annual report, product revenue was reported as $510,800,000. International revenue accounted for approximately 28 percent of net revenue for 1997. Therefore, we estimate domestic product revenues at $510,800,000 $\times$ .72 = $367,776,000, of which 60 percent were derived from network security:

$$\$367,776,000 \times 0.40 = \$220,665,600.$$

Julie Hawkins from investor relations provided the data on the breakdown of revenues (telephone conversation on November 19, 1998).

Retail Security (electronic article surveillance)

With 24 percent of market sales, Sensormatic Corporation is an industry leader in the electronic article surveillance industry. Sensormatic had revenues from domestic sales in 1997 of $448,000,000 (company annual report). We can, therefore, estimate total expenditures in the United States in 1997 on electronic article surveillance at

$$\$448,000,000 \ / \ .24 \ = \ \$1,866,666,667.$$

Vault Doors (financial institutions)

According to Richard Whipple (a sales representative for Diebold Corporation) the price of their high-end vault door is approximately $12,500. The cost of their low-end doors is approximately $10,500. We assume an average price of approximately $11,500. This figure includes installation and delivery. The number of financial institutions in the United States was identified in the *Statistical Abstract of the United States, 1997* (Tables 783 and 784) as 93,868. We assume that each institution has one vault door. At the average price of $11,500 per door, if these vault doors all had been purchased in 1997, the cost can be estimated as 93,868 × $11,500 = $1,079,482,000. On a straight-line, 25-year depreciation for the doors, the estimated resource expenditure that we assign to 1997 is $1,079,482,000 /25 = $43,179,280.

Armored Car Services

In 1997, revenues of the Armored car industry were approximately $1.2 billion. These figures were provided by John Dunbar in a telephone interview on October 15, 1998. Dunbar is the owner of Dunbar Armored, the third largest armored car company in the United States.

Investments by Private Parties to Perpetrate *Illegal* Wealth Transfers

Inasmuch as we cannot determine the value of specific resource investments made by would-be criminals in their pursuit of involuntary (from the victims' standpoint) wealth transfers, it must be estimated indirectly. Our general approach is to assume that criminals are indifferent between investing in legal versus illegal transfers for which the rates of return (defined broadly to include monetary and nonmonetary returns) are identical. That is to say, would-be criminal entrepreneurs will invest resources at the margin until the expected return from their activity exactly equals the expected return from investing in legally acceptable activity. If we know the rate of return to legally permissible activity, both productive and redistributive, we can apply the rate of return to the value of transfers perpetrated and work backward to obtain estimates of the resources expended to obtain the transfers.

The reported numbers with respect to the dollar value of transfers occurring during robbery, larceny/theft, burglary, and motor vehicle theft are found in *Crime in the United States, 1997*, U.S. Department of Justice, Federal Bureau of Investigation, Uniform Crime Reports. We note in passing that the reported numbers apparently understate the true magnitude of theft in America as not all crimes are reported. This suggests that our estimate in this regard likely understates the true magnitude of resource investment by thieves and would-be thieves.

Crime	Reported No.	Reported Total Losses
Burglary	2,461,120	$3.3 billion
Robbery	497,950	0.5
Larceny/theft	7,725,470	4.5
Motor vehicle theft	1,353,707	7.0
Total	12,038,247	$15.3 billion

The number of persons arrested for each category of crime is reported in the Federal Bureau of Investigation publication *Crime in the United States, 1998* (Table 30). The information on conviction rates (in 1994) and average jail time convicted offenders were sentenced to (in 1994) for each category of crime was taken from the FBI's *Sourcebook of Criminal Justice Statistics, 1997* (Tables 6.47 and 6.68, respectively).

Crime	Reported No. ×	No. Arrested =	Arrest Rate ×	Conviction Rate =	Probability of Going to Jail
Burglary	2,461,120	245,816	.100	.807	.087
Robbery	497,950	94,034	.188	.755	.1419
Larceny/theft	7,725,470	1,033,901	.133	.821	.1092
Motor vehicle theft	1,353,707	116,052	.085	.821	.0698

We assume that the opportunity cost of serving time in jail is equal to the minimum wage (i.e., that the individual would otherwise be employed full-time in a minimum wage job). The aggregate risk investment implicitly undertaken by individuals who perpetrate one of these types of crimes is found by multiplying the probability of going to jail by the average jail time an offender is sentenced to (in months), then multiplying this number by the total number of reported occurrences and then by the individual's forgone monthly earnings based on the $4.75 per hour minimum wage in effect for most of 1997 (the minimum wage was raised to $5.15 effective September 1, 1997).

Crime	Probability of Going to Jail ×	Avg. Jail Sen- tence ×	Forgone Earnings per Month ×	Occur- rences =	Implied Risk Investment
Burglary	.0807	27 mos.	$836	2,461,120	$ 4,483,078,700
Robbery	.1419	55	836	497,950	3,248,905,600
Larceny/theft	.1092	19	836	7,725,470	13,400,081,000
Motor vehicle theft	.0698	23	836	1,353,707	1,816,829,700
Total					$22,948,895,200

We have assumed that these individuals' hourly earnings would have remained constant and equal to the minimum wage for the entire period of the jail sentence. However, it seems possible, if not likely, that the typical individual's wage would rise during a 19, 23, 27 or, especially, 55 month period of time. To the extent that individuals would have earned more than the minimum wage, our estimation procedure understates the true (if implicit) resource investment by criminals in committing robberies, burglaries, and theft. We note that this investment comes predominately in the form of distortion to the labor market. It is also worth noting that our estimated implicit time investment by would-be thieves (nearly $23 billion) exceeds the total value of stolen property ($15.3 billion) by 50 percent. Seemingly, thieves are putting more at risk than they gain. This seems unlikely, on two counts. First, some number of burglaries, robberies, and thefts simply go unreported. Second, while we know, and therefore report, the value of the property affected by the reported robberies, burglaries, and thefts, we do not know the value of the property that would-be thieves *hoped* would be affected.

40

4. Resource Expenditures to Effect/ Prevent *Indirect* Transfers

Introduction

A significant portion of all redistributive activity in the United States each year involves the state, defined broadly to include all levels of government (federal, state, local), all branches of government (legislative, executive, judicial), and elected representatives as well as appointed bureaucrats. By virtue of statutory law or judicial interpretation, public sector employees are able to pass laws and regulations and make decisions that effectively take wealth, sometimes directly, sometimes indirectly, from one or more individuals and bestow wealth on others. The most overt mechanism for accomplishing this result is, of course, taxation. Governments at all levels use tax revenues to support programs that individual taxpayers may object strenuously to. Many of these public sector transfers are quite explicit and well-known:

- welfare programs that distribute cash or cash equivalents to identified individuals
- Social Security
- Workers Compensation
- state support for the arts
- Medicare and Medicaid
- agricultural commodity programs that pay farmers not to grow crops
- financial support for family planning clinics
- subsidies to American-based firms to advertise their products abroad

- construction of "public works" projects to the benefit of construction firms, construction unions, sports team owners, and so forth

Other state-provided transfers are in-kind and/or less obvious. Nonetheless, they transfer wealth from one segment of the population to another. Again, taxes provide the deus ex machina for the transfers to take place. Examples include

- school lunch programs
- publicly funded education
- discounted admissions for senior citizens into state-owned parks, zoos, and other sites
- myriad federal and state crop price-support programs
- race-, gender-, ethnicity-, or disability-based quotas for public sector contracts or benefit programs
- programs that provide free trees for landowners to plant
- programs that reimburse landowners for digging ponds on their property

Many additional public sector transfers are accomplished without the use of taxes, through state regulation of the terms and conditions under which business may be conducted. For example, the zoning board decision to ban nude dancing in a nightclub ultimately takes wealth (or well-being) away from the owner(s) of the nightclub, the dancers, and the patrons, and increases the wealth (or well-being) or those nearby neighbors who, for any of a number of reasons, might be adversely affected by the proximity of such a business. Other transfers are sought specifically through the judicial branch, drawing on the common law regarding torts, division of marital assets, and so on. Examples of these general types of indirect transfers include

- Requirements that electric power companies and telecommunications companies offer service to high-cost customers at below-cost rates that are "cross-subsidized" by low-cost customers who pay above-cost rates:

- Americans With Disabilities Act
- Family and Medical Leave Act
- Anti-discrimination laws
- Regulations that adversely affect an individual's use of his property, ostensibly for the "public good." For example, wetlands regulations and the Endangered Species Act permit the state to severely restrict the uses to which an individual may put private property, thereby effectively taking value, in most cases without compensation.
- Publicly enforced labor cartels, such as compulsory unions
- State regulations that restrict entry into certain occupations (e.g., law, dentistry, medicine, hairdressing, taxicab driving, and numerous others), creating artificial shortages of personnel, with the result that consumers pay higher prices
- Any regulation that restricts the import of foreign goods into the United States
- Legal protection from creditors via bankruptcy
- Tort litigation
- Contested divorce
- Legal requirements that gasoline contain a minimum concentration of ethanol, a corn-based alcohol—a regulation that artificially increases demand for corn grown in the Midwest, thus providing tens of millions of dollars in additional profits for midwestern corn farmers.[1]

In this chapter, we identify expenditures made by individuals who seek to use the power of the state to transfer wealth *indirectly* from others to themselves and expenditures made by individuals who seek to *prevent* such state-ordered transfers from occurring. We identify two principal categories of resource expenditures: (1) investments by private parties to perpetrate and/or prevent *legal* wealth transfers, and (2) investments by the state to perpetrate *legal* wealth transfers.

Investments by Private Parties to Perpetrate and/or Prevent *Legal* Wealth Transfers

POLITICAL ACTION COMMITTEES, 1977–1998 146,203,101

LOBBYISTS
National	$ 2,357,075,000
State	5,165,990,910

TORT LITIGATION
Lawyers and legal expenses	$ 91,500,000,000
Time-cost of contesting parties	Not able to determine

CONTESTED DIVORCE
Settled out of court	$ 846,256,950
Resolved at trial	297,553,550
Time	281,027,320
Subtotal	$ 1,424,837,820

BANKRUPTCY
Personal
Chapter 7	$ 820,512,000
Chapter 13	459,993,000
Time	1,900,800,000

Business
Chapter 11	$ 13,243,824,000
Subtotal	$ 16,425,129,000

UNIONS
Strikes (based on number of production days idle, 1997)	$ 310,472,880

ENTRY INTO RESTRICTED OCCUPATIONS 5,768,460,000

FEDERAL/STATE TAX LOOPHOLES
Tax Industry—Contracted Preparation	$ 8,923,076,923

Time
Individuals	$ 6,356,042,600
Businesses	35,328,800,000
Subtotal	$ 50,607,919,523

Investments by the State to Perpetrate *Legal* Wealth Transfers

ANTI-SMUGGLING
Customs, border enforcement	$ 2,450,000,000
International narcotics control	193,961,793
Drug Enforcement Administration	970,388,000
Subtotal	$ 3,614,349,793

INTERNAL REVENUE SERVICE
Tax compliance and enforcement	$ 4,091,220,000

U.S. DEPARTMENT OF JUSTICE
Antitrust division	92,447,000
TOTAL	$176,014,166,677

Sources

Political Action Committees, 1997–1998. These expenditures taken from the Center for Responsive Politics: (www.crp.org/lobbyists/industry).

LOBBYISTS

The resource investment in lobbyists has two components: the cash that changes hands and the couriers that transport that cash from interest groups to politicians. We estimate both expenditures:

The Cash

Expenditures at the national level by lobbyists in 1997 totaled $1,213,400,000 (this figure was taken from the Center for Responsive Politics Web site: www.crp.org). Expenditures at the state level by lobbyists in 1996 were approximately $819,727,560. That estimate was derived as follows:

Contributions to candidates for state political offices in 1996 for selected states are published by The National Institute on Money in State Politics (www.followthemoney.org). As reported, contributions to state political candidates were

Alaska	$ 6,597,446
Arizona	5,340,238
California	181,933,909
Colorado	4,024,923
Connecticut	3,608,932
Georgia	11,151,594

Idaho	2,526,533
Illinois	66,115,439
Indiana	10,030,007
Kansas	5,730,667
Kentucky	6,542,659
Maine	2,793,690
Michigan	12,491,090
Minnesota	7,219,472
Missouri	7,712,795
Montana	2,692,070
Nevada	6,851,984
New Hampshire	747,457
North Carolina	6,603,883
Ohio	26,324,097
Oregon	4,197,976
Rhode Island	938,135
Tennessee	4,032,835
Utah	1,707,719
Vermont	514,265
Washington	27,950,054
Wyoming	509,419
TOTAL	$425,889,288

The population of these 27 states in 1996 was 137,807,000. On a per capita basis, then, lobbyist spending on state politics in these states can be calculated by dividing aggregate lobbyist spending in these states by the combined population of these states:

$$(\$425,889,288 / 137,807,000) = \$3.09.$$

Assuming this general expenditure pattern also is characteristic of the unlisted states, we estimate *total* expenditures at the state level by multiplying $3.09 by the total population of the United States in 1996:

$$\$3.09 \times 265,284,000 = \$819,727,560.$$

The Couriers (lobbyists)

The number of registered lobbyists at the state level in 1996 was 43,703 (Council of State Governments). We assume that the typical lobbyist earns, on average, the same amount per year as the average lawyer ($99,450). Therefore, we estimate the labor cost of lobbyists registered at the state level in 1996 by multiplying 43,703 × $99,450 = $4,346,263,350.

The number of registered lobbyists at the national level in 1997 was 11,500, as estimated by Mr. Allan Shuldiner, with the Center for Responsive Politics (telephone conversation on April 21, 1999). Again, we assume that the typical lobbyist earns, on average, the same amount per year as the average lawyer ($99,450) and estimate the labor cost of lobbyists registered at the national level in 1997 by multiplying 11,500 × $99,450 = $1,143,675,000.

TORT LITIGATION
For the derivation of this number, see text, pp. 56–58 of this document.

CONTESTED DIVORCE
Information on the number of total divorces in 1997 (1,163,000) was provided by the National Center for Health Statistics (telephone conversation on November 6, 1998). Auburn, Alabama, attorney Beverlye Brady suggested that approximately 50 percent of divorces are uncontested (telephone conversation on February 12, 1999). This figure is roughly consistent with the percentage of families (58%) with children under age18 in1997 (*Statistical Abstract of the United States, 1997*, Table 67). We suspect that most divorces that involve children younger than 18 are contested, at least to some degree, and that some divorces that do not involve children are contested. Although we concede that many factors contribute to the likelihood that at least one party to a divorce will contest, the presence of children under the age of 18 surely is a significant indicator. We assume that 90 percent of contested divorces are resolved through out of court settlement, with the remaining 10 percent actually going to trial.

On the basis of conversations with Mrs. Brady, we assume that the average amount of money spent on attorneys' fees by both parties (added together) to a contested divorce that settles prior to trial is $1,617 and that the average amount of money spent on attorneys' fees by both parties to a contested divorce that goes to trial is $5,117. Thus, the total expenditure on attorneys' fees for contested divorce is estimated as

Contested and settled prior to trial:
$$523,350 \times \$1,617 = \$846,256,950$$
Contested and resolved at trial: $58,150 \times \$5,117 = \$297,553,550$

We further assume that the cases resolved out of court absorb an average of 20 hours of both the petitioner's and the defendant's time and that the cases taken to trial absorb an average of 100 hours of both the petitioner's and the defendant's time, valued in all cases at $8.63 per hour (median pay of wage and salary workers in 1987). The implicit investment by parties to contested divorces of their valuable time is thus estimated as

Settled out of court:
$$1{,}163{,}000 \times 0.5 \times 0.9 \times \$8.63 \times 40 = \$180{,}660{,}420$$
Resolved at trial:
$$1{,}163{,}000 \times 0.5 \times 0.1 \times \$8.63 \times 200 = \$100{,}366{,}900$$
Total time cost: $\$281{,}027{,}320$

BANKRUPTCY

Information regarding the number of bankruptcy filings taken from U.S. Courts Administrative Office. (Bankruptcy filing fees was provided by Judy Proctor, U.S. Courts Administrative Office, Bankruptcy Division (telephone conversation on February 11, 1999). The estimated legal fees were provided by Cecil Tipton, an attorney in Opelika, Alabama (telephone conversation on February 12, 1999). These fees represent his educated guess of the fee structure for the eastern division of the middle district of Alabama. No doubt, the fees in other states differ; our suspicion is that the fees in other states are higher than the fees in Alabama.

	1997 Filings	Filing Fee	Time	Legal Fees
Personal	1,267,200			
Chapter 7 (70%)	887,040	175.00	100 hours	$ 750
Chapter 13 (30%)	380,160	160.00	100 hours	$1,050

We have no way of knowing how much time the typical individual spends planning, preparing, and administering his/her personal bankruptcy situation. It is simply indisputable that there is, in fact, such investment of time that otherwise could be put to productive employment. While we have guestimated that the "typical" individual who files for Chapter 7 or Chapter 13 bankruptcy spends 100 hours of time in this regard, we concede that this number may be significantly inaccurate. However, we are confident that, if anything, this figure is conservative. We value individuals' time in alternative employment conservatively at $15 per hour. At this valuation, the implied time-cost of nonbusiness bankruptcy actions equals [1,267,200 × 100 × $15] = $1,900,800,000. The aggregate filing and legal costs equal

Chapter 7:   [887,040 × ($175 + $750)]   = $820,512,000
Chapter 13:   [380,160 × ($160 + $1,050)] = $459,993,000

	1997 Filings	Filing Fee	Time	Legal Fees
Business				
Chapter 11	52,800	$830.00	2,000 hours	$50,000

As with personal bankruptcies, individuals invest considerable time in the planning and execution of Chapter 11 bankruptcies. Indeed, it surely is the case that a number of significant people are involved in this process for any given filing. For example, the firm's chief executive officer and chief financial officer almost certainly are involved to the tune of hundreds of hours each. No doubt, other staffers are involved as well. Moreover, equivalent personnel from creditors surely are involved in the restructuring negotiations. To our knowledge, there is no reliable source of information about these time investments. We suggest that, on average, 5 individuals from the firm filing for Chapter 11 protection and 15 individuals from creditors spend 100 hours each per filing and that each of these individuals is compensated at a rate of $100 per hour. This implies a time-cost equivalent to [52,800 × 20 × 100 × $100] = $10,560,000,000. We concede the arbitrariness of our estimate but, again, believe that it likely understates the true time-investment by the affected parties.

Filing and legal fees add an additional [52,800 × $50,830] = $2,683,824,000 worth of cost for a total cost of Chapter 11 bankruptcies of $13,243,824,000.

These numbers are consistent with information provided by Ed Flynn, in the Executive Office for U.S. Trustees (telephone conversation on February 22, 1999). He indicated that explicit legal fees (i.e., not counting the time-costs) for Chapter 7, Chapter 11, and Chapter 13 bankruptcy filings came to approximately $3 billion in 1997.

UNIONS

Strikes

Strike-related work stoppages led to 4,497,000 idle production days in 1997 (Bureau of Labor Statistics Data, Series ID: WSU001).

Median hourly earnings of employed wage and salary workers in 1996 were $8.63 (*Statistical Abstract of the United States, 1997*, Table 675). Assuming an eight-hour workday, the implicit expenditure on strikes is estimated as:

$$\$8.63 \text{ per hour} \times 8 \text{ hours per day} \times 4{,}497{,}000 \text{ lost days} = \$310{,}472{,}880.$$

ENTRY INTO RESTRICTED OCCUPATIONS

States restrict entry into variety of professional and other occupations (e.g., taxicab drivers, beauticians, medicine, law, plumbing, etc.). A minimum estimate of individuals' monetary investment in securing access to these occupations may be formed by looking at the aggregate occupational licensing fees collected by the states. The information that we report was taken from the U.S. Census, *State Government Tax Collections: Fiscal Year 1996–97* (www.census.gov/govs/statetax/97tax.txt). However, because entry into these occupations is artificially restricted, the occupations typically are associated with higher pay and other compensation than would otherwise be the case. Consequently, individuals' occupational choices are influenced, with resulting distortions in labor markets that we are, unfortunately, unable to explore in this analysis.

FEDERAL/STATE TAX LOOPHOLES

Tax Industry

According to Brian Schell (investor relations, telephone conversation on November 3, 1998), H&R Block Inc. reported revenues of $1.16 billion for fiscal year 1998. The company did work on 14.8 million federal income tax returns (of a total 113 million filed). That gives H&R Block a 13 percent market share in their industry (23 percent of the tax returns are done by CPAs, 43 percent are done by self-preparers, 11 percent are done by other tax preparers, and the remaining 10 percent are done by friends for friends or family for family). Therefore, the total tax preparation industry had revenues of approximately $8,923,076,923 in 1997.

Time

Scott Moody at the Tax Foundation (telephone conversation on November 17, 1998) provided a summation of the hours spent per form by individuals and businesses in 1996. The total hours spent by individuals on tax forms and schedules in 1996 was 736,505,509. The total hours spent by businesses on tax forms and schedules in 1996 was 1,766,439,628. We assume that the average individual taxpayer's time can be valued at the median hourly pay for wage and salary workers in the United States ($8.63) and value the time spent by business(wo)men at $20 per hour. The implied time investment in tax preparation is calculated as follows:

$$736,505,509 \times \$8.63 = \$6,356,042,600\text{---individuals}$$
$$1,766,439,628 \times \$20.00 = \$35,328,800,000\text{---businesses}$$

Investments by the State to Perpetrate *Legal* Wealth Transfers

ANTI-SMUGGLING

Customs, Border Enforcement

This figure was provided by U.S. Customs Service employee Mark Harris (telephone conversation on November 10, 1998).

International Narcotics Control

According to U.S. Department of State employee Scott McAdoo (telephone conversation on November 12, 1998), the Department of International Narcotics and Law Enforcement Affairs had budget resources of $236,726,546 in 1997, of which they spent $193,961,793.

Drug Enforcement Administration

This information was provided by Drug Enforcement Administration employee Van Quarrels (telephone conversation on November 16, 1998).

INTERNAL REVENUE SERVICE

Tax Compliance and Enforcement

This information was provided by Internal Revenue Service employee Thad Juszczak (telephone conversation on February 11, 1999). The 1997 tax law enforcement appropriation was $4,091,220,000.

U.S. DEPARTMENT OF JUSTICE

Budget figures for the Antitrust Division of the U.S. Department of Justice were provided by Budget Office employee Bill Spencer (telephone conversation on October 28, 1998).

Notes

1. During the 1996 presidential election the Republican nominee, Senator Bob Dole of Kansas, rather shamelessly proclaimed himself "Senator Ethanol."

5. Why So Little Observed Rent-Seeking?

Introduction

The political economy of using the public sector to effect direct and indirect wealth transfers is well understood not only by special interest groups, politicians, and bureaucrats (the demanders and suppliers of special interest legislation) but also by an increasing number of private citizens and groups, most notably Public Choice economists. The expenditure of resources by potentially affected parties seeking to influence state-sponsored wealth redistributions is termed "rent-seeking." To economists, a rent is a value imparted by scarcity. Rents can occur naturally, as is the case when a young model earns enormous sums by virtue of her or his physical beauty. Beauty is scarce and therefore may impart scarcity rents (or value) to individuals who have the good fortune to be blessed genetically with attractive physical features. Indeed, those rents, defined broadly to include monetary and nonmonetary returns, evidently are sufficiently large to induce individuals who have not been blessed genetically with attractive physical features to invest significant sums of time and money undergoing plastic surgery to enhance their physical appearance.[1] When there is an expected positive return to be had from an investment, individuals invest accordingly.

Rents also can be contrived or artificial, as happens when the government uses its powers to restrict competition for certain firms in an industry. While the elimination of competitors does not change the market demand for the item being produced, it does make the quantity produced by the protected firm(s) more scarce relative to market demand than in the absence of such protection. This permits the protected firms to raise prices, at least to some extent, and implies a wealth transfer from consumers to the protected producers. Producers who would like to pad their bottom line at the expense of consumers will find it in their interest to lobby Congress and state legislatures for protection against competitors. The seeking of such favors from the state is rent seeking.

What is not well-known is the empirical relationship between the size of the rents to be had and the aggregate amount of resources spent to obtain or prevent the transfer. We illustrate the problem by example. Suppose that Congress is considering passage of a law that would severely restrict the importation of steel produced in foreign countries. The short-run effects of such a law are fairly easy to predict: higher prices charged by domestic steel producers, paid for by users of steel products. On the margin, the cost of steel will rise slightly. In turn, the cost increase will be felt by consumers in the form of higher prices for retail products that contain steel. In short, the law generates a wealth transfer from domestic steel consumers to domestic steel producers.

Let us suppose further that the discounted present value of the wealth transfer to domestic steel producing firms equals $10 billion. It surely is the case that the prospect of enriching themselves to the tune of $10 billion is sufficiently attractive to domestic steel producers that they would take steps to have such a law enacted. One relevant question is, How much will domestic steel producers spend to get such a law passed? In theory, they should be willing to spend up to $10 billion, less a normal rate of return, to obtain the transfer.

However, since consumers will lose at least $10 billion, they (collectively) have an incentive to oppose the transfer. This opposition may be focused through highly visible consumer action groups or occur when producers of consumer goods (such as automobiles) that use steel as an input object to import restrictions on steel because higher input prices imply higher costs and therefore lower profits. The point is, those from whom wealth may be taken have a financial incentive to fight the proposed transfer.

Coming to Grips with the Magnitude of the Problem

There is an increasing awareness in America of the fact that individuals *do* invest their time, energy, and other resources to effect favorable wealth transfers, to the detriment of society as a whole. After bearing witness to three decades of fraud and gaming of the system associated with President Johnson's Great Society, the American public rightly concluded that government-sponsored welfare programs have had enormous and far-reaching private and social costs. Jonathan Rauch (1994) and Donald Barlett and James Steele (1998) expose the massive magnitude of federal handouts to America's corporate special interests and the incestuous political relationship between politicians and the firms on which they lavish so many billions of taxpayer dollars. Stephen Moore and Dean Stansel (1995, 1996) have issued deserved criticism of both President Clinton and the Republican-controlled Congress for failing to live up to their respective promises to cut corporate welfare. The hypocrisy of our putative political leaders who publicly proclaim victory in the aftermath of their cuts in welfare for the poor while not cutting and, in many cases increasing, welfare for the rich, is simply astounding.

In many cases, we have been able to measure these investments directly. The size of the numbers undoubtedly will shock certain readers. There may be a tendency to disbelieve the figures. For example, is it really possible that Americans spent over $2 *billion* to influence politicians' votes with wealth transfer implications in 1997? The truth is that Americans indisputably spent much more than $2 billion; this number refers only to traceable expenditures on lobbyists. In addition, individuals spent time and money contacting politicians directly and indirectly (through the lobbyists). We are not able to measure these investments. We report that individuals paid more than $5 billion in 1997 in occupational licensing fees.

These labor cartels restrict the number of practitioners in their respective occupations, driving up the prices charged by those who are able to secure licensure. But the resource investment by individuals seeking to join a licensed occupation far exceed the license fee itself. There are educational courses to take, examinations to pass, forms to file, and the like, all of which cost petitioners substantially more, in the aggregate, than the licensure fees. Is it really the case that avoiding taxes has become a $50 *billion* plus annual industry in America? Absolutely—and, again, this number reflects only what we can measure and/or estimate with some confidence. We have no way of calculating the distortions in labor and capital throughout our economy that result from attempts to minimize taxes paid.

Unmeasured Investments Related to Arranging/Preventing Forced Wealth Transfers

In fact, our numbers grossly understate the magnitude of the resource expenditure in 1997 incurred in transferring, as opposed to creating, wealth in America. There is much that we have not even reported, because we were simply unable to measure investments that we are certain took place. For example, we know that individuals ''invest'' resources to secure transfers paid under private and commercial insurance. They get inflated estimates for car repairs and make exaggerated claims of medical or other damage from accidents. We know that individuals fake injuries and permit their job skills to atrophy in order to collect welfare from state and federal agencies. The list of these types of explicit or implicit investments is a long one.

Although we cannot measure such resource investments/distortions directly, we can speculate about their magnitude by examining the size of the transfers themselves, which we do know. For example, the Coalition Against Insurance Fraud estimated that insurance claims fraud in 1997 amounted to $79.9 billion.[2] If individuals expended as little as, say, 10 cents' worth of time, effort, money, risk, and so on for every dollar collected fraudulently from insurance companies, the implied resource investment in 1997 would have approached $8 billion.

This leads us to a question of no small importance: How much will all potentially affected parties invest, in the aggregate, to influence whether or not the $10 billion transfer occurs?

The fact is that no one knows the answer to this question. Indeed, what little we can glean from direct observation suggests that relatively small investments of cash are associated with extremely valuable political favors being granted, in the form of redistributions from one group to another. For example, we observed in chapter 4 that approximately $1.4 billion was spent in 1997 on political action committees (PACs) and lobbyists operating at the federal level. Yet the amount of money transferred in 1997 by Congress under the auspices of direct transfer programs was $1.11 trillion—nearly 1,000 times that much.[3] Additional wealth transfers, to the tune of many tens of billions of dollars, take place at the state and local levels. A case in point is the $10.5 billion spent by state and local governments in 1997 on economic development incentives—tax breaks and other programs designed to attract firms to locate in certain communities or to induce existing firms not to leave for other locations.[4] As nearly as we can tell, the recipient firms typically invest very little to obtain the taxpayer-funded giveaways.

Moreover, the amount of wealth transferred indirectly via government regulations likely exceeds, perhaps considerably, the wealth transferred via direct transfer programs. According to Richard Vedder (1996), government regulation has a detrimental effect on economic growth in the United States. He argues that the long-run economic consequences of government regulation are far greater than indicated by analysis of compliance costs only. Not only are economic resources (e.g., labor and capital) devoted to implementing regulatory mandates, they are used in a *less efficient manner* because the mandates force firms to allocate labor and capital differently than they would in the absence of the mandates. Vedder estimates that in 1994 the total cost of regulation in the United States was approximately $1.87 trillion ($1.27 trillion in output loss, another $600 billion or so in compliance costs).[5] Although Vedder's figures refer to wealth destroyed rather than wealth transferred by government regulations, our point is that his figures likely provide some indication of the aggregate magnitude of the indirect transfers at stake from the perspective of industries affected by government regulations. It seems doubtful that even the most crooked of politicians are willing to destroy nearly $2 trillion worth of economic wealth to effect a few paltry wealth transfers for campaign contributors or friends. Surely these very sizable compliance and opportunity costs reflect indirectly the enormity of the wealth transfers being effected by regulation.

Finally, we note that what is really at issue is the amount of wealth that *could be transferred* annually by federal and state legislatures. A single change in the federal tax code (e.g., a change in the capital gains tax rate) would affect the wealth of millions of individuals and firms, to the tune of many billions of dollars in the aggregate. This being the case, why do we observe so little overt rent-seeking in the public sector?

Why So Little Observed Rent-Seeking?

Part of the answer to this question involves the dynamics of rent-seeking itself. Individuals from whom wealth might be taken have a natural incentive to take action to prevent this from occurring. If the reader concedes this point, it is natural to follow up by asking why we don't observe more fighting over proposed political transfers of private wealth. Several complementary factors bear on the answer to this question. First, it apparently is the case that individuals are less opposed to having their wealth appropriated if they expect that money to be spent on what they perceive to be a noble cause than if they expect it to be spent on handouts to rent seeking sycophants. That is, taxpayers are not as likely to vote for a tax increase that they know will be distributed as massive subsidies to a handful of peanut farmers as they are to vote for an identical tax increase that supports "a cherished way of life in America." Not surprisingly, rent seekers have learned to disguise their grab for our money behind a cloak of public interest rhetoric. The wolf dons the sheep's clothing.

Second, individuals and special interest groups who engage in rent-seeking behavior typically are small, focused, and well organized. Suppose that five firms in an industry stand to gain (and evenly split) $500 million in additional profits per year from a passage of a federal subsidy program. Under the circumstances, each firm has $100 million worth of incentive to work actively to "encourage" legislators to support passage of the legislation creating the subsidy. We can be reasonably certain that this is sufficient financial incentive for each of the potentially affected firms actually to spend money to achieve the desired result. By contrast, the subsidy is paid out of general tax revenues. The fact that most taxpayers will be essentially ignorant with respect to the existence and/or effects of the subsidy minimizes the likelihood that significant opposition to the proposed subsidy will be mounted in the first place.

But the argument for noninvolvement of potentially adversely affected parties runs deeper. Let us suppose that every consumer in America knows perfectly well that the proposed subsidy program will personally cost 5 cents per week in higher prices for the subsidized commodity (e.g., milk, peanut butter, sugar, corn). How many of the millions of affected consumers are going to march on Washington to protest the loss of $2.60 per year? We suspect that not many will find it in their interest to do so. Special interest groups seeking political favors understand that they can minimize opposition to their proposed wealth transfers not only by disguising them as being in the public interest, but also by proposing to transfer small amounts of money from a large number of individuals. Not only is the personal financial incentive to oppose the proposed transfer minuscule, the free-rider problem looms large. That is, no one takes action in opposition to the putative transfer because each adversely affected individual hopes to free-ride on the efforts of whoever might muster such a challenge.

In addition to being able to disguise her motives and to maximize the number of others whose wealth she can attempt to appropriate, there is yet another particular advantage to Smith of using legislative and/or judicial surrogates to effect forced transfers from Jones: the state conveniently makes state-sponsored takings legal, albeit against the wishes of those whose wealth is appropriated. This minimizes the personal risk assumed by Smith in her quest to appropriate Jones' wealth.[6]

These dynamics of the rent-seeking process notwithstanding, we believe that the focus on how small the overt investments in rent seeking are relative to the size of the wealth transfers that occur is misleading, for two reasons. First, many of the overt investments often are difficult to trace. We expect robbers, burglars, and thieves to take pains to hide their activity from prying eyes, as they are subject to penalties imposed by the state. The fact that forced transfers are sponsored by the state (and thus immune from overt prosecution) does not imply that seekers of forced transfers brazenly flaunt their investment to obtain those transfers. Second, the mere fact that we do not observe dollars changing hands does not mean that investments are not being made. Other investments are less obvious than spending on PACs and lobbyists but far larger in magnitude: the time investments made by would-be politicians and members of special interest groups, the time investments made by individual citizens, and distortions in labor and capital markets. Money may not be, and apparently is not, the critical coin of investment with respect to securing or preventing publicly ordered transfers. Votes are the critical payoff to politicians who are positioned to arrange wealth transfers. Money is merely an instrument that helps politicians produce votes.

Non-Cash Investments in the Rent-Seeking Process

Professional scholarship on participation in the political process tends to focus on national elections to the exclusion of state and, especially, local elections. For many proposed wealth redistributions, it does pay voters to become politically informed and involved. A half dozen vocal homeowners protesting a proposed variance from a zoning ordinance that would permit someone to build an apartment complex next to them in Auburn, Alabama, carry a lot of weight with the local Planning Commission. The casting of (all) votes by citizens concerned with passage of (un)favorable legislation, ordinances, and so on implies a definite investment of their time in becoming knowledgeable about proposed transfers, and transmitting their preferences about any such proposed transfers to politicians and bureaucrats. Arguably, the value of this time investment is quite substantial.

Based on information reported in the *Encyclopedia of Associations* (Schwartz and Turner, 1995), associations claimed membership of approximately 300 million individuals and firms in that year. Obviously, some fraction of these individuals and firms were members of multiple associations. At least 20 percent of these associations devote some attention to transfer issues, as judged by the explicit description of their interests and/or activities in the *Encyclopedia* listing. If we assume a random relationship between size of organization membership and organization attention to transfer issues, then roughly 60 million association members are revealed to have a current interest in transfer activity. Admittedly, the actual time investments by individuals are unknown. It may be useful, however, to speculate about the magnitude of time investments made under plausible assumptions.

Suppose that a mere 5 of every 100 (5 percent) of these 60 million interested parties spend 10 hours per week reading up on relevant issues, writing newsletters, writing letters, developing Internet sites, composing and sending e-mail messages, attending hearings and meetings, and so forth. Suppose that an additional 20 percent of these interested parties devotes one hour per week to such activity and that the remaining 75 percent devotes one hour per month to such activity. At a time cost equal to the median hourly earnings of wage/salary workers in 1997 ($8.63—*Statistical Abstract of the United States, 1997*), the estimated implicit investment by association members with a revealed interest in transfer activity equals $23,508,120,000. There is an additional time cost associated with the many tens of thousands of hours of testimony presented in (sub)committee hearings at the federal and state levels, and before local planning commissions and zoning boards each year.

In at least one respect, the figures with respect to investments by association members in the transfer process are understated. The maximum time investment per week was assumed to be 10 hours. In addition to this relatively low-level time investment by organization members, there is the administrative apparatus of the organization itself. For those organizations/associations that owe their entire existence to transfer activity, 100 percent of their activities (and expenditures) arguably represent wasted resources, as we have defined waste earlier. Examples include the American Association for Affirmative Action ($160,000 budget), the Association for Children for Enforcement of Support ($623,000 budget), the American Safe Deposit Box Association ($130,000 budget), the American Society for Industrial Security ($8,000,000 budget), and the National Burglar and Fire Alarm Association ($1,800,000 budget). There are, of course, many others for which budget information is not reported (e.g., the International Association for Shopping Center Security, the Security Industry Association, the Retail Loss Prevention Association, and the Locksmith Security Association).

We can investigate the matter (of implicit investment of time) further by estimating the time expenditure by voters on transfer-related issues. Specific figures with respect to the number of individuals who voted in the national elections in 1996, as well as the voting age population and the number of registered voters in that year (*Statistical Abstract of the United States, 1997*, Tables 437, 462, and 464) are:

- Number of individuals who voted—96,273,000
- Number of individuals of voting age—196,509,000
- Percentage of individuals of voting age who registered to vote—65.9.

We assume that each individual who voted did so only after investing in acquisition of a certain amount of information about relevant forced transfer possibilities (among other aspects of the decision calculus). Furthermore, it is arguable that those who register to vote but do not actually vote, and even those who do not register, have an interest in promoting favorable and preventing unfavorable state-ordered wealth transfers, and therefore undertake some investment in obtaining information about transfer possibilities. For all three groups, we suspect that the time investment is substantial, in the aggregate. Sources of information about transfer possibilities and consequences include, but are not limited to the following: local, state, and national newspapers, television news broadcasts, radio programs, news magazines, discussions with friends and/or individuals with shared interests, and Internet sites. There were over 9 million subscribers to *Time* magazine, *Newsweek*, and *U.S. News and World Report* in 1997. The circulation of daily newspapers in 1997 exceeded 50 million. Of the 100 million households in the United States in 1997, nearly 100 percent had at least one television, with average total household viewing time per day equal to 9.6 hours per household.

Clearly, these sources provide much information that is not related to viewer-specific transfer activity. However, constant attention is required to keep abreast of transfer possibilities, especially those that might be unfavorable, for two reasons. First, to the extent public choice theory correctly predicts that small, well-organized special interest groups can (and will) successfully use the political process to forcibly transfer wealth in their favor from large, diffuse populations, the typical individual will rationally expect, on average, to be a victim of forced transfers more frequently than (s)he benefits from forced transfers. Second, individuals do not know *when* efforts to take their wealth unfavorably will be undertaken, and thus they must constantly be on guard against them.

Given the volume of election coverage by the media and the extent to which individuals consume information provided via newspapers, news magazines, the Internet, and television implied by the previously identified sources, as well as the unknown, but nonetheless positively valued, quantity of time spent discussing transfer aspects of political decisions made at all levels of government with co-workers, family, friends, and similarly situated individuals, we can speculate about the total amount of time "invested" by citizens to influence wealth transfer activity via the vote coin. On the assumption that an individual who votes invests an average of one-half hour per day on acquiring information relevant to casting appropriate votes, and that those who register but do not vote and those who are eligible to vote but do not register invest an average of 5 minutes per day on acquiring information about transfer activity, the implied investment cost per year in 1997 was approximately *$150 billion.*[7] This number is, without question, highly speculative. Nonetheless, it serves a useful purpose: to underscore the magnitude of the time commitments we make relative to possible wealth transfers. Indeed, it seems to us that the true time expenditure could be much larger than what we suggest, but is not likely to be much smaller.

On top of this investment in acquiring knowledge about proposed transfer activity, citizens must make their preferences known to the political agents who have the power to (not) effect specific transfers. These expenditures also are potentially large in magnitude. In Auburn, Alabama, for example, the city council, the planning commission, and the school board meet once each month. On average, the city council meetings run approximately 90 minutes, and the meetings of the planning commission and school board run about an hour. Each committee has 7 members and each meeting is attended, on average, by approximately 10 non-member citizens. In the city of Auburn alone, this represents an implied annual time investment in attending preference-revealing meetings equal to 714 hours. Assuming that the ratio of the number of citizens expressing preferences per capita is roughly constant across political jurisdictions, and that each local political jurisdiction has, on average, the three committees mentioned above (i.e., that Auburn is a "representative" town), the estimated time investment for all county, municipal, and township governments in the United States in 1997 was approximately $9 billion. The time cost of registering and voting in local, state, and national elections (at least in even years) comes to an additional several hundred million dollars.

State-arranged wealth transfers, especially regulatory edicts and social mandates, create significant distortions in labor and capital markets. Although most of us are dimly aware of these distortions, the true magnitude and scope of the distortions are exceedingly difficult to measure. We know, for example, that every workplace in America has had to spend money and resources to provide "reasonable" accommodation for "disabled" individuals. At Auburn University, there is a dedicated office, with a full-time staffer and secretary, to help provide wealth transfers to individuals identified as disabled. There is a dedicated office containing special equipment to assist disabled students. The equipment alone must have cost many tens of thousands of dollars; heaven only knows how (in)frequently the equipment gets used. It is a safe bet that the manufacturer(s) of this equipment were solidly behind the push to gain passage of the Americans With Disabilities Act. The pro rata cost of the office space surely amounts to additional tens of thousands of dollars. Moreover, every faculty member in colleges and universities across America now expends time and effort to provide special conditions for disabled individuals that are not available to other students. Even if such efforts cost each faculty member only one hour per year, the total represents tens of millions of dollars worth of forced transfers of faculty time. There are firms whose very existence is based on the need of larger firms to have minority subcontractors to even compete for federal government contracts. There are publications and staffing agencies that specialize in identifying and reaching minority candidates for jobs. States and localities subject to court-ordered racial representation among teachers and administrators in public schools and colleges expend hundreds of thousands of dollars annually to such entities. Auburn University staffs an Equal Employment Opportunity (EEOC) compliance office that absorbs many thousands of dollars worth of resources each year. Every other major college in America spends resources similarly. So do the major corporations and public agencies, if not on specific EEOC personnel, then in learning what is required to comply with various statutory and judicial provisions.

We do not here contest the underlying social imperative. Perhaps there is strong societal agreement to transfer wealth to groups based on their racial, sexual, ethnic, physical, or mental characteristics. The fact remains that the transfers, as currently configured, are enormously costly, by virtue of the distortions in labor and capital markets that result. The economic cost of the individuals and firms involved in administering these wealth transfers are figured, at least partially, into our current accounting of gross domestic product (GDP). However, the individuals and expenditures do not create new wealth for Americans; they reflect transferred wealth only.

Although we cannot trace the vast majority of distortions to labor and capital markets caused by transfer activity, we can estimate one that is sizable and of interest, because it illustrates the fundamental point we seek to make—the misallocation of labor into the legal profession. We estimate the number of lawyers engaged in transfer, as opposed to productive, activity in 1997 as follows. In 1997, the combined GDPs of the countries belonging to the Organization for Economic

Cooperation and Development (OECD) equaled $22,176.0 billion.[8] The GDP of the United States in 1997 was $7,824.0 billion (35.3 percent of the OECD total). There were roughly 1.2 million lawyers in the world in 1997, of whom approximately 880,000 were practicing in the United States (*Statistical Abstract of the United States, 1997*). By subtraction, the number of lawyers practicing in countries other than the United States in 1997 was approximately 320,000. We assume that all non-U.S. lawyers practice in the OECD countries, and that transfer activities in these countries do not involve lawyers. That is, we explicitly assume a purely productive role for lawyers outside of the United States.[9] The non-U.S. OECD countries had a combined GDP of $14,352 billion in 1997. Each non-U.S. lawyer is thus associated with $14,352 billion/320,000 = $44,850,000 in GDP.

We assume the truly productive value of U.S. lawyers equals the productive value of non-U.S. lawyers. We can therefore divide GDP in the United States in 1997 by $44,850,000 to obtain an estimate of the number of productive lawyers in the United States in 1997: 174,448. The number of lawyers that are (by implication) not engaged in productive economic activity is determined by subtracting the number of lawyers estimated to be contributing to productive economic activity (174,448) from the total number of lawyers in the United States (880,000). Our admittedly rough estimate, then, is that perhaps four out of every five lawyers in the United States owe their existence to involvement in transfer activity rather than productive activity.

Our information with respect to average annual earnings of lawyers in 1997 was provided by Altmann & Wiel, Inc., of Ardmore, Pennsylvania, who routinely conduct survey research for the American Bar Association. Average total compensation in 1997 of associates (partners) in private practice was $86,421 ($216,715). Assuming that partners constitute one-tenth of private practice attorneys, overall average annual compensation is approximately $99,450. We estimate the labor market resource distortion implied by lawyers whose practice is due to their involvement in transfer activity by multiplying the number of lawyers engaged in transfer activity by average annual compensation:

$$705,552 \times \$99,450 = \$70,167,146,000.$$

Of course, lawyers are not the only input in the production of legal services. There are offices, telephones, office equipment, paralegals, secretaries, supplies, and so forth. In 1996, 1,303,000 individuals were employed in the legal services industry (*Statistical Abstract of the United States, 1997*, Table 649). We know that approximately 880,000 of these individuals were lawyers. Of the 423,000 others, 281,000 were identified as legal secretaries and 113,000 paralegals (*1998–99 Occupational Outlook Handbook*). Average annual earnings of paralegals in 1995 are recorded as $32,900 plus a bonus of $1,900 (National Federation of Paralegal Associations). Average annual earnings of executive secretaries, whom we take to include legal secretaries, were $30,823 in 1990 (*The American Almanac of Jobs and Salaries 1990–91*). Even with low inflation, we can reasonably expect that figure to have risen to approximately $35,000 by 1997. Assuming that the fraction of legal secretaries and paralegals that are engaged in unproductive transfer activity mirrors the fraction previously determined for lawyers (four out of five), we can estimate the size of the labor resource distortion among legal secretaries and paralegals as

legal secretaries: $281,000 \times 0.8 \times \$35,000 = \$7,868,000,000$
paralegals: $113,000 \times 0.8 \times \$34,800 = \$3,145,920,000$

Taken together, our estimate of the labor market distortion in the legal services sector of the economy because of forced transfer activity comes to over $81 billion. This estimate, rough as it may be, is remarkably consistent with an alternative estimate. *Total* expenditures on legal services in 1995 came to $114.4 billion (*Statistical Abstract of the United States, 1997*, Table 1288). Following the earlier pattern, we assume that 80 percent of these expenditures are derived from legal involvement in redistributive activity. This implies that roughly $91.5 billion in 1995 (a little more in 1996) was spent on redistributive (i.e., unproductive) legal activity. The difference between the $81 billion labor distortion and the $91.5 billion total distortion represents capital equipment, supplies, and other resource expenditures.

Having made the basic point about transfer activity creating enormous distortions in the deployment of economic resources in the U.S. economy, it should be clear that we could, at least in principle, analyze the distortions in other labor markets (e.g., accountants) and in capital markets (e.g., the implications of subsidies to businesses for individual taxes across states).

Notes

1. Nonmonetary forms of the rents associated with beauty might include the ability to attract a more desirable (defined broadly) mate, looks, comments, and diverse indications that others appreciate (value) one's appearance, and career opportunities that otherwise might not be available. Of course, the more of this sort of investment that takes place, the more common becomes physical beauty, which in turn decreases the marginal value associated with the attribute. We note that the multi-billion-dollar cosmetics and skin care industry exists by virtue of many millions of individuals investing to capture expected rents associated with beauty.

2. A document faxed to the authors by the C.A.I.F. identified the specific categories as follows: auto—$13.9 billion, homeowner's—$2.1 billion, business/commercial—$9.8 billion, and health—$53.9 billion. These figures do not include costs related to detection, investigation, or prosecution of insurance fraud and do not include any estimate of the amount of fraud committed by insurers or those purporting to be in the business of insurance.

3. This figure was developed from information taken from the U.S. Department of Commerce, Bureau of Economic Analysis Web site (www.bea.doc.gov/bea/newsrel/pi0399), Table 1—Personal Income.

4. Our source for this number was National Association of State Development Agencies spokeswoman, Nancy McCray (telephone conversation on April 5, 1999). She estimated expenditures by the states on incentives for business development at between $9.9 billion and $11.1 billion in 1997. For purposes of our estimate, we took the midpoint of McCray's numbers. This estimated investment includes loans and tax incentives (i.e., forgone revenues) but does not include direct project funding like buildings, streets, railroad spurs, and so forth. Loans and tax incentives typically are provided

over a number of years; the figure reported to us by McCray is the NASDA estimate of the amount of investment in 1997, not the capitalized value of incentives granted in 1997 but that extend into the future.

5. The latter number is consistent with the estimate developed by Hopkins (1996).

6. In his *Selected Essays on Political Economy*, Frederic Bastiat (1995) provides a superb example (pp. 25–26) of the way seekers of special protections and privileges use the apparatus of the state to minimize risk to themselves:

> Mr. Protectionist (it was not I who gave him that name; it was M. Charles Dupin) devoted his time and his capital to converting ore from his lands into iron. Since Nature had been more generous with the Belgians, they sold iron to the French at a better price than Mr. Protectionist did, which meant that all Frenchmen, or France, could obtain a given quantity of iron with less labor by buying it from the good people of Flanders. Therefore, prompted by their self-interest, they took full advantage of the situation, and every day a multitude of nailmakers, metalworkers, cartwrights, mechanics, blacksmiths, and plowmen could be seen either going themselves or sending middlemen to Belgium to obtain their supply of iron. Mr. Protectionist did not like this at all.
>
> His first idea was to stop this abuse by direct intervention with his own two hands. This was certainly the least he could do, since he alone was harmed. I'll take my carbine, he said to himself. I'll put four pistols in my belt, I'll fill my cartridge box, I'll buckle on my sword, and, thus equipped, I'll go to the frontier. There I'll kill the first metalworker, nailmaker, blacksmith, mechanic, or locksmith who comes seeking his own profit rather than mine. That'll teach him a lesson!
>
> At the moment of leaving, Mr. Protectionist had a few second thoughts that somewhat tempered his bellicose ardor. He said to himself: First of all, it is quite possible that the buyers of iron, my fellow countrymen and my enemies, will take offense, and, instead of letting themselves be killed, they might kill me. Furthermore, even if all my servants marched out, we could not guard the whole frontier. Finally, the entire proceeding would cost me too much, more than the rent would be worth.
>
> Mr. Protectionist was going to resign himself sadly to just being free like everyone else, when suddenly he had a brilliant idea.
>
> He remembered that there is a great law factory in Paris. What is a law? he asked himself. It is a measure to which, when once promulgated, whether it is good or bad, everyone has to conform. For the execution of this law, a public police force is organized, and to make up the said public police force, men and money are taken from the nation.

If, then, I manage to get from that great Parisian factory a nice little law saying: 'Belgian iron is prohibited,' I shall attain the following results: The government will replace the few servants that I wanted to send to the frontier with 20,000 sons of my recalcitrant metalworkers, locksmiths, nailmakers, blacksmiths, artisans, mechanics, and plowmen. Then, to keep these 20,000 customs officers in good spirits and health, there will be distributed to them 25 million francs taken from these same blacksmiths, nailmakers, artisans, and plowmen. Organized in this way, the protection will be better accomplished; it will cost me nothing; I shall not be exposed to the brutality of brokers; I shall set iron at my price; and I shall enjoy the sweet pleasure of seeing our great people shamefully hoaxed.

7. Of course, individuals watch television or read magazines or newspapers for reasons (e.g., entertainment) other than to acquire information about possible wealth transfers. Consequently, the information obtained could be regarded as being a byproduct of engaging in other activities and therefore not costly. However, an individual is not *compelled* to spend his time reading every article written in the local paper he reads each day. He is not *forced* to read the published agendas for upcoming planning or zoning commission meetings, which occasionally include proposals that affect his well-being. The fact that he deliberately takes the time (which could be spent on other valuable pursuits) to read such inclusions in the newspaper (or whatever media sources he consumes) suggests that his acquisition of this information is not a byproduct of reading for entertainment but, rather, the result of purposive investment of his time.

8. These countries include Australia, Austria, Belgium, Canada, Czech Republic, Denmark, Finland, France, Germany, Greece, Hungary, Iceland, Ireland, Italy, Japan, Korea, Luxembourg, Mexico, Netherlands, New Zealand, Norway, Poland, Portugal, Spain, Sweden, Switzerland, Turkey, United Kingdom, and United States.

9. As we use foreign lawyers per capita in the OECD countries as a basis for estimating the number of socially "productive" lawyers in the United States, the fact that we assume a purely productive role for all lawyers in OECD countries implies that our estimate of the extent of involvement by U.S. lawyers in forced transfer activity is conservative. If, for example, we had assumed that the equivalent of one-half or one-third of OECD lawyers' time is spent on transfer-related activity, this would have lowered OECD ratio of productive lawyers per capita which, in turn, would have increased our estimate of the number of lawyers engaged in transfer activity in the United States.

6. Concluding Comments

We conclude our investigation by noting that the numbers we present clearly understate the magnitude of resource expenditure on transfer activity in the United States. For example, we were not able to develop a reliable estimate of commercial expenditures on locks. Such expenditures would include the cost of locks for commercial buildings, churches, hotel rooms, offices, and desks. Similarly, we do not have an estimate for expenditures on locks (on buildings, offices, desks, etc.) at all levels of the public sector. We do not have expenditures for theft detection/prevention from libraries. Aside from the up-front expenditure for the theft detection equipment and installation, there is continuing expenditure for the power to operate the equipment, the sensing strips installed in new acquisitions, the employees' time spent installing these strips, and employees' time spent desensitizing materials that are checked out. Citizens purchase Mace and other products to help prevent robberies. They build homes and equip ground-floor apartments with iron bars across the windows to deter burglars. Again and again, we are aware of expenditures made but for which we have no numbers.

Indeed, even the numbers we do report understate the true magnitude of the problem. For example, one of the investments that unions make to improve their bargaining position with respect to firms is calling a strike. A strike burns up union members' time, on which we can place a value. But the ultimate resource expenditure extends well beyond the lost productivity of the strikers—it encompasses the lost or reduced productivity of everyone else whose productivity depended, directly or indirectly, on the productivity of the strikers.[1] Likewise, the tax abatement and direct incentives offered to businesses to persuade them to locate in specific communities almost inevitably influence the resulting tax structure for the private citizens and remaining businesses located in those communities. In addition, ripple effects in demand for local services such as schools, waste collection and treatment, etc., affect the community. We have not spoken to these issues in our analysis.

Many hundreds, if not thousands, of local, state, and federal programs redistribute wealth indirectly. For example, it has been charged that some activist groups use the Community Reinvestment Act to extort wealth transfers from (ultimately the stockholders of) financial institutions. As has become painfully obvious in recent years, individuals and groups sometimes base lawsuits or complaints to the Equal Employment Opportunity Commission on racial, sexual, or other putative discrimination in attempts to redistribute wealth from "deep-pocket" firms to themselves. While we can identify and report budgets for these agencies, it is extraordinarily difficult to know how much is being invested in attempts to effect such wealth transfers and attempts to either forestall such wealth transfers or to minimize those that occur.

We reiterate a point made earlier—we do not care about how socially "worthy" such programs may be. The "rightness" or "wrongness" of wealth transfers is utterly immaterial to our findings regarding the magnitude of the resource expenditures to obtain them. The fact is that government programs redistribute wealth, and, consequently, individuals will expend resources to influence the extent to which this occurs, one way or another. People may be offended at the suggestion that individuals invest in obtaining/maintaining transfers under government programs such as Supplemental Security Income; low-income housing subsidies; the food stamp program; benefits for sufferers of black lung disease, AIDS, cancer, and so forth. Transfers may result from special interest group activity or from some broad "social" consensus; they are still transfers and they are still costly. Consider the introductory quote by

Gordon Tullock—transfers do not simply occur, they must be produced at some investment cost that consists of the resources spent by all potentially affected parties in influencing the transfer outcome. These expenditures permanently reduce a society's production possibilities (real well-being and growth) from what would be experienced in the absence of the transfer activity.

The numbers that we report make it abundantly clear that the production possibilities frontier for the United States would shift out considerably if individuals (and the state) were not in the transfer business. Responsibility for the implied drain on our economy is multitiered. At an elemental level, the responsibility lies with individual members of our society. We covet our neighbors' and fellow citizens' wealth and have precious few qualms about using the courts or legislatures to get it. With respect to the former, ambulance-chasing lawyers are not the culprit, despite the black hats they are depicted in the popular press as wearing. Contingency fee lawyers would not be in the transfer business if individuals like us were not in the transfer business. As the cartoon character Pogo put it so succinctly many years ago, "We have met the enemy and he is us."

But the problem is yet more complex. The institutional structure of both legal rule-making and judicial decision-making creates incentives that encourage redistributive entrepreneurship. There is no question but that interest groups lobby legislators for special wealth enhancements taken from taxpayers. In this context, the supply of statutory wealth transfers may be regarded as demand-driven, with members of legislatures playing an essentially passive role as suppliers of forced transfers. However, there is convincing evidence that, far from being passive in this process, legislators and bureaucrats actively extort money and other compensation from the business community by threatening to impose regulatory costs (McChesney, 1997).

The occasional threat from Washington to regulate prices charged in the funeral home industry is a case in point.

"Concerned" politicians voice dismay at the pricing policies in the industry and suggest that federal price controls may be "essential" to ensuring "fair" treatment of consumers in their "time of need." This is followed fairly immediately by a surge in campaign contributions to members of the House of Representatives and Senate, especially those who sit on the relevant committee(s), by representatives of the funeral home industry. Then the talk of price-gouging dies down until it is time for Congress to shake down the industry again.

The editors of the *Wall Street Journal* (November 8, 1999, A50) were especially pointed in their identification and criticism of the extortive motives behind the antitrust prosecution of Microsoft:

> But let's get to the real bottom line. Washington's crusade against Microsoft has fulfilled its purpose, serving as a great lever to pry open the wallets of Silicon Valley. Where three years ago the technology plutocrats spent their surplus income on racing yachts and Ferraris and charity, now they patriotically send donations to Washington to support the fixer class and its retinue in the style to which it would like to become accustomed.

The fact that plaintiffs may join class-action suits against so-called deep pockets firms without being required to demonstrate actual harm case by case creates strong incentives for individuals who have not suffered harm to join such suits, simply to get in on the forced wealth transfer. The fact that punitive damages are awarded to plaintiffs (and their lawyers under contingency fee arrangements) creates enormous incentives for individuals to bring tort actions and for lawyers to encourage the filing of such actions.

What to Do?

It seems doubtful that individuals' desire to promote their self-interest will change any time soon. Indeed, we certainly hope that it does not. As we indicated at the beginning of our essay, individuals acting in furtherance of their self-interest can create an enormous amount of good for everyone else in society. However, we know that there is a dark side to self-interest, in the form of attempts to appropriate the wealth of others, so any attempt to mitigate the harmful effects of such activity must focus on structural changes. For example, punitive damages are awarded to plaintiffs in addition to compensatory damages in tort cases despite the fact that punitive damages do not make the plaintiff indifferent between suffering no damage and suffering damage that is compensated. Thus, the awarding of punitive damages to plaintiffs provides enormous financial incentive for plaintiffs to seek wealth transfers through tort litigation. A simple structural change would radically reduce the incentive: de-link punitive damages from compensatory damages.[2] Economic efficiency, as well as simple justice, demands that parties that have been injured by the (intentional or negligent) actions of others should be permitted to recover damages from the injurer(s) to make them whole. Insofar as punitive damages are socially desirable as a means of providing incentive for potential injurers to engage in the efficient level of potentially harmful behavior, burn the money. This creates efficient incentives for injured parties and for parties that engage in harmful behavior.

The point of this example is to emphasize our contention that simple structural changes are capable of significantly lowering the private payoffs to individuals from expending resources in pursuit of their neighbors' wealth. Such changes are the sine qua non of reversing the wave of redistribution-related resource expenditures now swallowing up a large fraction of public and private spending in the United States.

In addition to structural changes that reduce the ability of individuals to profit from engaging in redistributional activities, significant reductions in such activity also could be accomplished, in principle, by lowering the relative returns from stealing as opposed to honest, productive work. This might be accomplished, in part, by increasing our commitment as individuals to heaping opprobrium on those caught stealing, perpetrating welfare or insurance fraud, or engaging in any type of forced transfer activity. In turn, this would reduce the imperative for individuals to invest resources to protect themselves from having their wealth taken from them without their consent. We have suggested that, all other things equal, individuals are indifferent between profiting by stealing wealth from others and profiting by developing new products that others trade their wealth for voluntarily. Yet the choices actually made by individuals to maximize self-interest are of enormous consequence to society. Stealing is socially costly; new goods and services are socially beneficial. A revitalized social ethic that elevates productive work above stealing would, without question, create added value for all Americans.

Notes

1. Union leaders, of course, are well aware of this and, depending on circumstance, time strikes to maximize the economic leverage that can be exerted upon the firm(s).

2. This policy prescription was suggested by Auburn University economics professor Randy Beard.

References

Barlett, Donald L. and James B. Steele. 1998. "Corporate Welfare," *Time*, November 9, pp. 34–54.

______. 1998. "Fantasy Islands and Other Perfectly Legal Ways That Big Companies Manage to Avoid Billions in Federal Taxes," *Time*, November 16, pp. 79–93.

______. 1998. "Paying a Price for Polluters," *Time*, November 23, pp. 72–82.

______. 1998. "The Empire of the Pigs," *Time*, November 30, pp. 52–64.

Bastiat, Frederic. 1995. *Selected Essays on Political Economy*. Irvington-on-Hudson, N.Y.: Foundation for Economic Education.

Becker, Gary S. 1983. "A Theory of Competition Among Pressure Groups for Political Influence," *Quarterly Journal of Economics* 98 (August: 371–99).

Buchanan, James M. 1967. *Public Finance in Democratic Process*. Chapel Hill, NC: University of North Carolina Press.

Buchanan, James M. 1968. *The Demand and Supply of Public Goods*. Chicago: Rand McNally.

Buchanan, James M., and Geoffrey Brennan. 1980. *The Power to Tax*. Cambridge: Cambridge University Press.

Buchanan, James M., and Gordon Tullock. 1962. *The Calculus of Consent*. Ann Arbor, Mich.: University of Michigan Press.

Hopkins, Thomas D. 1996. "Regulatory Costs in Profile," Center for the Study of American Business. Policy Study No. 132 (August).

Jensen, Michael C., and William H. Meckling. 1976. "Agency Costs and the Theory of the Firm." *Journal of Financial Economics* 3: 305–60.

Insurance Information Institute. 1998. *1999 Fact Book*.

Laband, David N., and John P. Sophocleus. 1992. "An Estimate of Resource Expenditures on Transfer Activity in the United States," *Quarterly Journal of Economics* 107: 959–83.

McChesney, Fred S. 1997. *Money for Nothing: Politicians, Rent Extraction, and Political Extortion*. Cambridge, Mass.: Harvard University Press.

Mixon, Frank C., David N. Laband, and Robert B. Ekelund. 1994. "Rent Seeking and Hidden In-Kind Resource Distortion: Some Empirical Evidence." *Public Choice* 78: 171–85.

Moore, Stephen, and Dean Stansel. 1995. "Ending Corporate Welfare as We Know It." Cato *Policy Analysis* No. 225 (May 12).

______. 1996. "How Corporate Welfare Won: Clinton and Congress Retreat from Cutting Business Subsidies," Cato *Policy Analysis* No. 254: (May 15).

Off-Highway Research. 1998. *The Construction Equipment Industry in North America: Long-Term Machinery Forecast,1999*.

Peltzman, Sam. 1976. "Toward a More General Theory of Regulation," *Journal of Law and Economics*. 19 (October): 211–40.

Rauch, Jonathan. 1994. *Demosclerosis: The Silent Killer of American Government*. New York: Times Books.

Ravenal, Earl C. 1997. "The 1998 Defense Budget," Chapter 7 of the *Cato Handbook for Congress—105th Congress*. Washington: The Cato Institute.

Schwartz, Carol A. and Rebecca L. Turner. 1995. *Encyclopedia of Associations*, 29th Ed. Detroit, Mich.: Gale Research, Inc.

The American Almanac of Jobs and Salaries 1990–91. New York: Avon Books.

Tollison, Robert D. 1982. "Rent Seeking: A Survey," *Kyklos* 35: 575–602.

Tullock, Gordon. 1989. *The Economics of Rent Seeking and Special Privilege*. Kluwer Academic Press.

———. 1988. "The Costs of Rent Seeking: A Metaphysical Problem," *Public Choice* 57: 15–24.

U.S. Department of Commerce, Bureau of the Census. Various. *Statistical Abstract of the United States*. Washington: U.S. Government Printing Office.

———. 1996–97. *State Government Tax Collections: Fiscal Year 1996–97*. Washington: U.S. Government Printing Office.

U.S. Department of Justice, Federal Bureau of Investigation. *Uniform Crime Reports—1997*. Washington: U.S. Government Printing Office.

———. U.S. Bureau of Justice Statistics. 1997. *Sourcebook of Criminal Justice Statistics*,

Varian, Hal R. 1989. "Measuring the Deadweight Costs of DUP and Rent Seeking Activities." *Journal of Economics and Politics* 1.

Vedder, Richard K. 1996. "Regulation's Trillion-Dollar Drag on Productivity." Center for the Study of American Business, Publication No. 165 (March).

VGM Career Horizon. *1998–99 Occupational Outlook Handbook*. 1997. Lincolnwood, Ill.

Index

Americans with Disabilities Act, 65

Barlett, Donald, 11, 55
Bastiat, Frédéric, 70–71n6
Becker, Gary S., 9, 10
Buchanan, James M., 9

Clinton, Bill, 55
Community Reinvestment Act, 74
Competition, restricted, 53–54
Consumers
  choices of, 1
  of information, 62–63
  losses to, 7
  wealth transfers from, 54–55
Crime
  state investment to protect
    against organized, 22, 25
  state investment to protect
    against personal, 22, 26–27
  state investment to protect
    against white collar, 22, 26

Defense spending, 22, 27

Economic activity
  in absence of transfers, 74–75
  distortions caused by
    redistribution, 10, 18–19
  effect of regulation on, 57
  GDP overstates, 19
  incentives to undertake harmful,
    5–10
Ekelund, Robert B., 18
Equal Employment Opportunity
  Commission (EEOC), 66, 74
Exchanges, 12

Fiscal illusion
  cost of, 9–10
  occurrence of, 20n3

Government
  defense spending, 22, 27
  investment to protect against
    restraint of trade, 22, 27–28
  redistributive activity of, 41–43
  spending to effect or prevent
    wealth transfers, 1–3
  spending to perpetrate legal
    wealth transfers, 44–45, 51
  spending to protect against
    illegal wealth transfers, 22–25,
    28–38
  subsidies to for-profit
    corporations, 11
  See also Public sector; Regulation
Great Society, 55
Gross domestic product (GDP)
  cost to administer wealth
    trnsfers in, 66–67
  overstates economic activity, 19

Individuals
  incentives to acquire wealth of
    others, 5
  influence on distribution of
    income and wealth, 1
  influence on public policy by,
    17–18
  self-interest of, 76
  spending to effect or prevent
    wealth transfers, 1–3
Information
  about forced wealth transfers,
    63–64
  about spending by burglars, 11
Interest groups
  disguised motives of, 59–60
  engaged in rent-seeking, 59
  lobbying of, 75
  public choice theory predictions
    about, 63–64

Investment
   to obtain or prevent forced
      transfers, 1–2
Investments
   to influence potential wealth
      transfers, 55–56
   in redistributive activity, 10–11
   seeking favor of politicians and
      bureaucrats, 17–18
   in special workplace
      accommodations, 65–66
   See also Time investment

Jensen, Michael C., 20n2
Johnson, Lyndon B., 55

Laband, David N., 18

Market distortions, 65–69
Meckling, William, 20n2
Mixon, Frank C., 18
Moore, Stephen, 20n4, 55
Mueller, Dennis, ix

Peltzman, Sam, 20n1
Politicians
   as extortionists, 75–76
   incestuous relations with firms,
      55
   role in forced wealth transfers, 7
   seeking favors from, 17–18
   spending to influence votes of,
      55, 60
Private sector
   spending to perpetrate and/or
      prevent
   legal wealth transfers, 44–51
   spending to perpetrate illegal
      wealth transfers, 25, 38–40
   spending to protect against
      illegal wealth transfers, 22–25,
      28–38
   See also Individuals
Property rights
   private investment to protect
      private, 22–25, 28–38
   spending to define and enforce,
      9, 14–16

   voluntary and involuntary
      transfer of, 14–16
Public choice theory, 63
Public sector
   Social Security, 74
   transfer programs of, 41–42, 74
   wealth transfers by, 41–52, 55
   welfare programs of, 55–56

Rauch, Jonathan, 55
Redistribution
   distortions caused by, 18–20
   incentives for, 73–74
   social cost of, 6–10
   See also Transfers
Regulation
   total cost of (1994), 57
   wealth transfers in, 56–57
Rents
   contrived, 53
   naturally occurring, 53
Rent-seeking
   actions to prevent, 58–59
   defined, 53
   hidden, 58–60
   non-cash investments in, 61–69
   small investments for large
      wealth transfers, 57–58
   unavoidable spending of, 8–9
Rooney, Andy, ix

Self-interest, individual, 76
Social Security, Supplemental
   Security Income, 74
Stansel, Dean, 20n4, 55
Stealing as forced transfer, 5, 19n1
Steele, James, 11, 55
Subsidies to for-profit
   corporations, 11

Tax avoidance
   industry devoted to, 56
   market distortions with, 56
Time investment
   to influence wealth transfers, 1,
      64–65
   to learn about proposed wealth
      transfers, 62–64
Tollison, Robert, 8

Transfers
distortions in markets created
by, 65–69
to individuals with special
problems, 65–66
legal personnel involved in
activities related to, 66–69
organizations existing to make,
62
potential for, 58
private investment to perpetrate,
25–26, 38–40
by public sector, 41–52, 54
ratio of spending to size or
value of, 56–58, 62
under regulatory legislation,
57–58
spending to effect or prevent,
1–3
spending to influence, 17–18,
55–56

state-ordered, 8
See also Redistribution
Transfers, forced
definition of, 12
direct, 21
investment to effect or prohibit,
12
methods to effect, 5–6
private investment to perpetrate
direct, 25
private investment to protect
against direct, 22–25
social cost of, 6–10
spending to obtain or prevent, 1
using legislation for, 59
Tullock, Gordon, ix, 9, 10, 75

Varian, Hal, 19n1
Vedder, Richard, 57

Welfare programs, government-
sponsored, 55–56

About the Authors

David N. Laband is Professor of Forest Economics in the School of Forestry and Wildlife Sciences at Auburn University. He received his Ph.D. in economics from Virginia Tech in 1981. His professional research interests include the economic causes and consequences of government regulation, law and economics, and taxation. He is the author of 6 books and more than 70 refereed journal articles in a wide range of economics journals including the *American Economic Review*, the *Journal of Political Economy*, the *Quarterly Journal of Economics*, and the *Review of Economics and Statistics*. In addition, he writes extensively for nonacademic audiences, in outlets such as the *Wall Street Journal* and other major newspapers. He is a member of Auburn University's Forest Policy Center.

George C. McClintock works as a financial consultant with Salomon Smith Barney in Birmingham, Alabama. He graduated suma cum laude from Auburn University in 1999 with a degree in economics. He was the 1998 recipient of the Charles Anson Award for attaining the highest grade point average in economics at Auburn.

Cato Institute

Founded in 1977, the Cato Institute is a public policy research foundation dedicated to broadening the parameters of policy debate to allow consideration of more options that are consistent with the traditional American principles of limited government, individual liberty, and peace. To that end, the Institute strives to achieve greater involvement of the intelligent, concerned lay public in questions of policy and the proper role of government.

The Institute is named for *Cato's Letters*, libertarian pamphlets that were widely read in the American Colonies in the early 18th century and played a major role in laying the philosophical foundation for the American Revolution.

Despite the achievement of the nation's Founders, today virtually no aspect of life is free from government encroachment. A pervasive intolerance for individual rights is shown by government's arbitrary intrusions into private economic transactions and its disregard for civil liberties.

To counter that trend, the Cato Institute undertakes an extensive publications program that addresses the complete spectrum of policy issues. Books, monographs, and shorter studies are commissioned to examine the federal budget, Social Security, regulation, military spending, international trade, and myriad other issues. Major policy conferences are held throughout the year, from which papers are published thrice yearly in the *Cato Journal*. The Institute also publishes the quarterly magazine *Regulation*.

In order to maintain its independence, the Cato Institute accepts no government funding. Contributions are received from foundations, corporations, and individuals, and other revenue is generated from the sale of publications. The Institute is a nonprofit, tax-exempt, educational foundation under Section 501(c)3 of the Internal Revenue Code.

CATO INSTITUTE
1000 Massachusetts Ave., N.W.
Washington, D.C. 20001